PREFACE

This book has been in progress for some twenty-five years. It began with an idea that there was a void in the literature regarding the church in general and what has come to be called the "Black Church" or the "African American Church" in particular. Initially it was my view that to fill this void, a book needed to be written focusing on the psychology of the "Black Church." However, the more I read and studied the Bible, studied the science of psychology, researched history, observed the church community, participated in its activities, and read books and other literature, I felt that a book simply focusing on the psychology of the "Black Church" would be too limited. Rather, given the powerful historical and continuing influence of God and the church on the life, survival, and progress of Black people, I became convinced that the focus should be psychology *in and through* the "Black Church" in the context of the biblical tradition.

Therefore, the purpose of this book is to take a look through psychological and biblical lenses into the Christian church with a specific emphasis on the "Black Church." Use will be made of available literature and research, along with personal observations and reflections as a psychologist and Christian.

Faith in the God of the Bible and an association with the institutional church have had overall positive influences on the African American community and were key in the survival of the slave experience in America. The phrase "A Steady Beat" (in the title) is taken from what has come to be known as the Black National Anthem, "Lift Every Voice and Sing." This song epitomizes the struggles, hopes, resiliency, and aspirations of peoples of African descent in the Americas. Moreover, the phrase itself is very reflective of the role of the institutional church in the lives of peoples of African descent.

ACKNOWLEDGMENTS

I wish to thank the following persons for their assistance in reviewing and providing comments on various drafts of this work: my wife, Shirley Ann Spencer June (for both her counsel and invaluable assistance), Ms. Cynthia Ballenger, Dr. Bernard L. Richardson, Dr. Patricia Williams, Dr. Warren Williams, Dr. Michael Lyles, and Dr. Willie Richardson. Additionally, the work of Ms. Anna Yokoyama is appreciated for her valuable assistance in the editing, formatting, and occasional typing of parts of the manuscript.

INTRODUCTION

Through the eyes of one who is both a Christian and a trained psychologist, this book will examine both the positive impacts as well as aspects of the church, the Body of Christ, that need attention in order for its mission to be advanced more effectively. Moreover, it will take a specific look at and into the church with a focus on what has been labeled as the "Black Church" or the "African American Church." Overall, the evidence is overwhelming that the God of the Bible and the institutional church have been major positive factors in the lives of Black people in the Diaspora.

The terms "African American Church" and "Black Church" will be used interchangeably. By "Black Church" or "African American Church," I concur with the definition given by Lincoln and Mamiya (1990) in their book *The Black Church in the African American Experience*. Regarding the usage of the term, they stated:

> We use the term "the Black Church" as do other scholars and much of the general public as a kind of socio-

logical and theological shorthand reference to the pluralism of black Christian churches in the United States. Since the late 1960s "the Black Church" has replaced the older reference, "the Negro Church" which was used by scholars of a previous generation. In general usage any black Christian person is included in "the Black Church" if he or she is a member of a black congregation. In this study, however, while we recognized that there are predominantly black local churches in white denominations such as the United Methodist Church, the Episcopal Church, and the Roman Catholic Church, among others, we chose to limit our operational definition of "the Black Church" to those independent, historic, and totally black controlled denominations, which were founded after the Free African Society of 1787 and which constituted the core of black Christians. Today the seven major black denominations with a scattering of smaller communions make up the body of the Black Church and it is estimated that more than 80 percent of all black Christians are in these seven denominations, with the smaller communions accounting for an additional 6 percent (p. 1).

The seven historical denominations included under Lincoln and Mamiya's definition are:

- African Methodist Episcopal (A.M.E.)
- African Methodist Episcopal Zion (A.M.E.Z.)
- Christian Methodist Episcopal (C.M.E.)
- National Baptist Convention, U.S.A., Incorporated (NBC)
- National Baptist Convention of America, Unincorporated (NBCA)
- Progressive National Baptist Convention (PNBC)
- Church of God in Christ (COGIC)

Even though the essence of the definition of the "Black Church" as used by Lincoln and Mamiya is shared, whenever the term "Black Church" or "African American Church" is used in this work, it will be displayed in quotation marks. This is so because, although that description has good sociological and psychological usefulness, the convention was chosen because nothing can supersede the fact that the true biblical church is one.

This work will also include observations and reference to literature of all churches as well as predominantly Black congregations that fall outside of the seven historical Black denominations. For example, the Full Gospel Baptist Fellowship came into being in 1994 after Lincoln and Mamiya's publication.

Lincoln and Mamiya (1990) released their monumental work almost two decades ago. Since then, much remains the same, yet there are signs of new expressions of faith. These new expressions (phenomena) will also be explored.

This book is divided into five parts and contains twelve chapters. Part one is entitled "History" and contains two chapters, the first of which is a reflection on history as it relates to the formation of the "Black Church." The history chapter is followed by a review of the elements and goals of psychology and how western and Black psychologies differ in their views of the importance and role of religion.

Part two entitled "Typologies, Models, and Names" contains two chapters: one of which deals with types and models of churches and the other with types of members and what these mean to the overall functioning of congregations.

In part three, "Church Settings," the first chapter explores the contributions historically and contemporarily of the pastor and church setting in meeting the psychological needs of individuals. Then rituals, offerings, songs, and prayers are explored. Finally, because the impact of the church is so powerful in the lives of so many, several statements that are made within church settings that can have detrimental psychological effects on those attending are examined and discussed.

In part four, entitled "Counseling and Psychological Service Delivery," one chapter is devoted to a discussion of the general area of psychotherapy/counseling and the church. The second chapter in this section deals with the challenges and opportunities of counseling in the religious arena with a special focus on biblical counseling (an area and focus that is becoming increasingly popular).

In part five, entitled "The Church—Living up to Its Full Potential," the first chapter contains a discussion and reflection on the continuing potential of the church and what must be done to maximize this potential. The second chapter gives a perspective on what it will take to make the church as beautiful as are many of the buildings. The final chapter is a summary of suggested resources to assist the reader in maximizing one's own life as well as the potential of the church.

While the book focuses and draws heavily from the literature on the "Black Church," the basic concepts, ideas, and analyses are applicable to churches in general. A unique feature of this book is that it takes both a psychological and biblical (spiritual) perspective in its analysis of the materials presented and discussed.

It is my hope and prayer that this book will serve as a practical aid to the entire church community in becoming the "healing community" that is its tradition while simultaneously contributing to the scholarship on the church in general regardless of its local congregation's primary ethnicity.

PART 1
HISTORY

Reflections on the
History of the Church
with an Emphasis on
the "Black Church"

A Review of
Psychology and Religion—
Western and African Styles

CHAPTER 1

Reflections on the History of the Church with an Emphasis on the "Black Church"

"Take you up every man of you a stone upon his shoulder . . . That this may be a sign among you, that when your children ask their fathers in time to come, saying, What mean ye by these stones? Then ye shall answer them . . . and these stones shall be for a memorial unto the children of Israel for ever."

JOSHUA 4:5–7

"My people are destroyed for lack of knowledge: because thou hast rejected knowledge, I will also reject thee . . ."

HOSEA 4:6

"And hath made of one blood all nations of men for to dwell on all the face of the earth, and hath determined the times before appointed, and the bounds of their habitation."

ACTS 17:26

INTRODUCTION

A knowledge of and familiarity with history are essential. Such knowledge and familiarity allows one to properly place oneself in the world. History helps to define who we are and where we have been. Without an appreciation and understanding of history, an individual's significance on the world stage is warped and one cannot fully understand and appreciate one's place in and contributions to society. History allows us to connect with our past, navigate our present, and anticipate the future. Psychologically, history gives meaning to life and connects us with those who have gone before.

The importance of a proper education, which includes a clear sense of history, is undoubtedly one of the factors that motivated Carter G. Woodson to write the classic *The Miseducation of the Negro* (1933). Two quotes from him underscore the necessity for an understanding of history. For example, in the Introduction, he stated:

When you control a man's thinking you do not have to worry about his actions. You do not have to tell him to stand here or go yonder. He will find his "proper place" and will stay in it. You do not need to send him to the back door. He will go without being told. In fact, if there is no back door, he will cut one out for his special benefit. His education makes it necessary (p. xiii).

In the opening chapter, titled "The Seat of Trouble," Woodson stated:

The "educated Negroes" have the attitude of contempt toward their own people because in their own as well as in their mixed schools Negroes are taught to admire the Hebrew, the Greek, the Latin and the Teuton and to despise the African (p. 1).

The importance of history is also one of the factors that most likely motivated Molefi Asante (1988) to write extensively on "Afrocentricity." By Afrocentricity, Asante means that in any study of African people, Africa must be placed at the center. Specifically, he stated that "Afrocentricity is the belief in the centrality of Africans in post modern history" (p. 6). Thus without a proper anchoring in history, we end up seeing ourselves not as actors but pawns on the world stage. For a critique of the pros and cons of Afrocentricity as it applies to Black Christians, see June (1996).

History is well represented in the Bible. When a categorization of the books of the Bible is done, several of them are listed as history. Moses, as well as the patriarchs Abraham, Isaac, and Jacob, regularly reviewed aspects of history and recited it to the younger generations. Jesus Christ Himself valued history in His teachings as demonstrated by His references to the Law and the prophets.

I have increasingly come to appreciate that no matter what one's discipline or profession, there must be some working knowledge of history. Thus in this opening chapter, as a psychologist and Christian, I will present my understanding of history as it relates to the formation and continuation of the "Black Church." A brief review of history in this chapter, along with a review of the tools of psychology in the next, is necessary before we delve into our treatise of psychology and the "Black Church." Those who are interested in a deeper study of church history may wish to review, for example, the following sources: Woodson, 1921; Mays and Nicholson, 1933; Frazier and Lincoln, 1974; Lincoln and Mamiya, 1990; Raboteau, 2001; and Bingham, 2002.

Early Black Involvement with the God of the Bible and with Christianity

When considering what is called the "Black Church," a distinction must be made between the beginning of Black involvement with Christianity and the origin of the "Black Church" in America. Black involvement with Christianity existed from its inception. There are many references to Africa and ample evidence of Black presence in the Old Testament world. Works such as McCray (*The Black Presence in the Bible*, 1990a and 1990b) and Isichei (*A History of Christianity in Africa*, 1995) provide evidence of Black involvement in the Old Testament world. If one agrees, as many now do (see for example, McCray, 1990; Felder, 1993; and *Newsweek*, 1988) that the biblical Adam and Eve were of African origin (and hence Black), then Blacks were involved directly with God from the beginning. This is important to establish because these ancient incidents are the precursors to what has evolved into Christianity.

Since Christianity is a New Testament phenomenon, one can also find Black presence there. Often overlooked is the fact that, as a child, Jesus spent time in Africa, specifically Egypt (see Matthew 2:13–15). It is also known that Simon of Cyrene who was compelled to carry the cross of Jesus was of African origin (see Matthew 27:32). One likewise finds the presences of Black people on the day of Pentecost since African countries are referenced: "And there were dwelling at Jerusalem Jews, devout men, out of *every nation* under heaven. Now when this was noised abroad, the multitude came together, and were confounded, because that every man heard them speak in his own language" (Acts 2:5–6; italics mine). Specific locations are also mentioned: *"Phrygia, and Pamphylia, in Egypt, and in the parts of Libya about Cyrene"* (Acts 2:10, italics mine).

Moreover, one finds in Acts 8:26–39 an early conversion to the faith by a person of Ethiopian descent. The direct reference to him as being from Africa is found in verse 27 (italics mine): "And he arose and went: and, behold, *a man of Ethiopia,* an eunuch of great authority under Candace *queen of the Ethiopians,* who had the charge of all her treasure, and had come to Jerusalem for to worship."

These references from the New Testament are among those that clearly and unequivocally indicate early Black involvement with Christianity.

EXTRA-BIBLICAL SOURCES ON
EARLY BLACK INVOLVEMENT WITH CHRISTIANITY

Christianity runs deep in African history and there are many who have addressed this early Black involvement. Mbiti (1970), for example, noted:

Both Christianity and Islam are "traditional" and "African" in a historical sense, and it is a pity that they tend to be regarded as "foreign" or "European" and "Arab" (p. xiii).

Christianity in Africa is so old that it can rightly be described as an indigenous, traditional and African religion. Long before

22

the start of Islam in the seventh century, Christianity was well
established all over north Africa, Egypt, parts of the Sudan,
and Ethiopia. It was a dynamic form of Christianity, producing
great scholars and theologians like Tertullian, Origen, Clement
of Alexandria and Augustine. African Christianity made a
great contribution to Christendom through scholarship, participation in Church councils, defence of the Faith, movements
like monasticism, theology, translation, and preservation of the
Scriptures, martyrdom, the famous Catechetical School of
Alexandria, liturgy and even heresies and controversies (p.
300).

Regarding Christianity's early presence in Africa, in the
book *Introduction to African Religion*, Mbiti (1975) says:

Christianity, the religion which puts its faith in Jesus Christ,
came to Africa shortly after the death and resurrection of Jesus.
It is believed in Egypt that Christianity was first brought there
by St. Mark, one of the writers of the Bible, in the year 42 AD
(p. 182).

Mbiti (1975) goes on to say that:

This ancient African Christianity thrived and produced many
great leaders, thinkers and ideas in the Church. World Christianity benefited enormously from African Christians of the
first six or seven centuries . . . Ancient Christianity survived in
Egypt and Ethiopia, where it is found up to this day (p. 182).

Williams (1976) in the book *The Destruction of Black Civilization* also addressed early African Christian involvement, as
the following reveals:

> That Christian states were in Africa from the earliest times had not been completely forgotten . . . There was no reason why the ancient African Church should have been "forgotten" at all. The Vatican records and those at Constantinople were available (p. 267).

It is extremely important psychologically to recognize that Blacks were involved with Christianity long before the American sojourn in mass numbers because if we do not recognize the rich history of achievements prior to America, then we will have primarily a "slave mentality" and this can damage us psychologically.

By "slave mentality" I mean the belief that the Black experience in the world began in slavery and is totally shaped by that experience. A "slave mentality" will further cause us either to be unaware of, to dismiss, or to devalue the prior history of Black achievements as kings, queens, inventors, the builders of pyramids, contributors to religious systems, scientists, architects, the developers of great civilizations, and so on. Not only is it important psychologically to show this, but to do otherwise is to be historically inaccurate. Such accurate knowledge also deepens our sense of connection to the Christian movement.

CHRISTIANITY AND THE AMERICAN EXPERIENCE— THE ORIGIN OF THE "BLACK CHURCH" IN AMERICA

Ample evidence has been established in the Bible and from extra-biblical sources that Blacks worshiped the God of the Bible from the beginning and likewise were a part of Christianity from its inception. Further, given that Christianity may be considered traditional to Africa, what then is the evidence that some Africans brought to America were already Christians? This question will be examined below.

Speaking in reference to this issue, C. Eric Lincoln in the foreword to Wilmore's book (1973) said:

The Blacks brought their religion with them. After a time they accepted the white man's religion, but they have not always expressed it in the white man's way. It became the Black man's purpose—perhaps it was his destiny—to shape, to fashion, to recreate the religion offered him by the Christian slavemaster, to remold it nearer to his own heart's desire, nearer to his own particular needs. The Black religious experience is something more than a black patina on a white happening. It is a unique response to an historical occurrence which can never be replicated for any people in America (p. v).

Lincoln (1974) in the book *The Black Church Since Frazier* specifically commented on slaves as being already Christians when he said that: "It is possible that some slaves brought to this country were Christian" (p. 154). Later writers, as shall be shortly shown, are more emphatic in this claim than Lincoln.

Raboteau (1980) in his book *Slave Religion—The "Invisible Institution" in the Antebellum South* likewise believed that some slaves were exposed to Christianity prior to coming to America. Specifically, he stated: "Similarly, it is possible that a few enslaved Africans may have had some contact with Christianity in their homeland" (p. 6). However, in a later book *Canaan Land: A Religious History of African Americans*, Raboteau (2001) was more emphatic:

Africans, both free and slave, had arrived in Portugal and Spain through North Africa since the early Middle Ages. Many had learned the Europeans' languages and had accepted their religion. Reflecting their status as baptized Christians, they were called *ladinos*, (literally "latins," meaning Spanish or

25

Portuguese speakers). In fact, the first Africans in the Americas —some arrived as free people, some as slaves—were *ladinos*. Because *ladino* slaves developed a reputation for running away and encouraging Indians to rebel, Spanish authorities on Hispaniola requested that they be prohibited and that *bozales* (unbaptized, "uncivilized") slaves be sent instead. Although Muslim and Christian Africans were swept up in the Atlantic slave trade, the vast majority of those enslaved in the Americas practiced the traditional religions of their ancestors (p. 8).

Raboteau goes on to explain how the ancient African traditions and religions paralleled that of European Christians in their beliefs about the nature of the world, the meaning of human existence, etc. They both believed that God created the world, that He sustained everything in it, and that the one God existed in three divine persons.

Hence, consistent with historical evidence, it is more accurate to say that what happened when Blacks came to America; that is, were forcibly brought to America, was a broader exposure to Christianity and an exposure to it in the American form.

Therefore, "Black Church" development in America and the practice of religion by Blacks have been greatly influenced by the African past and is an amalgamation of African and American religious experiences. One sees evidence of this in worship styles, particularly in the early stages, in the form of "the dance," the treatment of the deceased, etc. For example, Wilmore (1973) states:

By the end of the middle sixteenth century some African slaves from the coast of Guinea had been introduced to Protestantism by Captain John Hawkins, the English privateer and adventurer. Since most of the first slaves to be brought to the American colonies came from the Antillean subregion, it is possible that some of them had already made a partial transition from their native religions to Christianity prior to any systematic evangelization on the mainland (p. 7).

Wilmore (1973) further observed:

The religion of Black people in the United States today, and in parts of the West Indies, Central and South America, is unquestionably predisposed to the beliefs and practices associated with Judeo-Christian tradition. But the Christianity which had been developing for more than four hundred years among the descendants of the first slaves brought to this part of the world is a different version of the religion that is professed by the descendants of the slavemasters. In recent years, particularly in the United States, Black theologians and historians have been uncovering this aboriginal "Black Religion" and have sought to indicate the points at which it not only differs from what most white people believe, but where it may illuminate some of the depths of man's most elemental religious consciousness which have been obfuscated by secularism and the technological development of Euro-American civilization (pp. 2–3).

Music within the "Black Church" is also influenced by the African tradition. This has been amply noted by Walker (1979) who stated that: "As music was central to West African culture, so is music central to the historic Black religious experience. This is another evidence of African survival" (p. 22).

While reflecting on the history of the "Black Church," it is critical to remember that what is called the "Black Church" is not an institution that was developed to stay away from Whites. Rather, slavery, the legacy of slavery, White supremacy, racism, and discrimination were the driving forces leading to its formation and

27

development. Speaking to this point, Dr. Martin Luther King Jr. (in Carson & Holloran, 1998) said:

> I say "so called Negro Church" because ideally there can be no Negro or white church. It is to their everlasting shame that white Christians developed a system of racial segregation within the church, and inflicted so many indignities upon its Negro worshippers that they had to organize their own churches (p. 73).

THE EXPERIENCE OF THE 16TH
THROUGH THE EARLY 19TH CENTURIES

Given that some Blacks who came to America had been exposed to Christianity before the slave trade period, during the 1600s and 1700s in the Americas, great efforts were made by such groups as the Quakers and the Society for the Propagation of the Gospel in Foreign Parts, as well as other individuals, to evangelize and "convert" Blacks on a large scale to American Christianity (Woodson, 1921; Turner, 1999).

Initially, therefore, both in the North and South, Blacks were members of and attended "White" churches, worshiped freely, and were a part of their associations (Woodson, 1921). However, as the number of Blacks increased in these "White" churches, special sections were established for Blacks in an effort to control "free worship." These sections that had been set aside were often called "Nigger heaven." This type of forced segregation and the inability to worship freely ultimately led to the formation of separate congregations and later separate denominations and associations. For example, in 1816 Richard Allen founded one such denomination, the African Methodist Episcopal Church.

Speaking to the issue of the formation of predominantly Black congregations, Low and Clift (1981) state:

During the latter half of the eighteenth century, the black Baptists began to establish independent churches in various parts of the country . . .

By 1814 a number of Baptist churches were composed entirely of Negro members—both freedmen and slaves; however, the majority of Negro Baptists were members of the same churches as their owners. Black churches were included in district associations along with white churches (p. 160).

Thus the "Black Church" as a distinct entity began to evolve on a large scale after the Richard Allen incident wherein he and Absalom Jones were physically removed from a predominantly White congregation while they were praying, which led to the formation of the Free African Society in 1787. Commenting on this situation, Low and Clift (1981) stated:

The development of the African Methodist Episcopal Church, the oldest organization of any kind established by Negroes in the United States, has passed through several phases. It originated in 1786 at Philadelphia as a small prayer band in St. George's Church under the leadership of Richard Allen (1760–1831). This group subsequently developed into the Free African Society in 1787.

With Allen was Absalom Jones, the founder and organizer of St. Thomas's Protestant Episcopal Church in 1794, also an outgrowth of the Free African Society . . . From the Free African Society also emerged the semi-independent Bethel Church, which later became completely autonomous and the organizing nucleus for the new denomination in 1816.

The singular fact that characterized the several African Methodist societies that met at Philadelphia in 1816 to form a unified body was their desire to be free from control and discrimination and to have wider and fuller expression in the total life of the church than had been available in the churches from which they had seceded . . .

It was following discrimination, together with gross personal indignities, that the sizeable group of blacks withdrew in a body from St. George's Church in Philadelphia in 1787 and formed the Free African Society (p. 32).

Hence these separate congregations became more and more identified as a unique institution and began to serve a variety of needs for Blacks: theological, political, economical, sociological, and psychological. When worship became severely restricted in the South, Blacks began to congregate into what some have called the "invisible institution." This "invisible institution" served as a place for Blacks to meet "freely," to maintain and create survival bonds, and to worship God secretly and away from the fear of retaliation by Whites. Raboteau (1980) speaking to the issue of the "invisible institution" states:

By the eve of the Civil War, Christianity had pervaded the slave community . . . At first glance it seems strange to refer to the religion of the slave as an invisible institution, for independent black churches with slave members did exist in the South before emancipation. In racially mixed churches it was not uncommon for slaves to outnumber masters in attendance at Sunday services. But the religious experience of slaves was by no means fully contained in the visible structures of the institutional church. From the abundant testimony of fugitive and freed slaves it is clear that the slave community had an extensive religious life of its own, hidden from the eyes of the master. In the secrecy of the quarters or the seclusion of the brush arbors ("hush harbors") the slaves made Christianity truly their own (p. 212).

There are records of "Black churches" in America that go back to the 1770s. It is generally believed that the first Black independent church in America was organized in Silver Bluff, South Carolina, between 1773 and 1775. During this period of time, the Black pastor/preacher also began to evolve into a unique personage.

Lincoln (1974) speaking to the origin of the "Black Church" stated:

> The Black Church had been born of the travail of slavery and oppression. Its very existence was the concrete evidence of the determination of Black Christians to separate themselves from the white Christians, whose cultural style and spiritual under-standing made no provision for racial inclusiveness at a level acceptable to Black people. Ever since Richard Allen and his Black fellow worshippers had been forcibly ejected from Philadelphia's St. George Methodist Church as they knelt in prayer in a segregated gallery, the resulting establishment of a separate Church had symbolized even at its beginning the Black American's commitment to dignity and self-determination (p. 107).

THE LATE 19TH AND EARLY PART OF THE 20TH CENTURIES

In spite of the Emancipation Proclamation that was issued in 1863, Blacks and Whites continued to live in separate societies. This separation was reinforced and later again institutionalized with the Plessey vs. Ferguson Supreme Court decision in 1896 declaring "separate but equal" the law of the land. As time

passed and with the institutionalization of Jim Crow laws, the
"Black Church" expanded and became an even more influential
institution within America and in the lives of Black people.

In the latter part of the 19th century, following the Emancipation Proclamation, Black colleges with a Christian base
were established. Heavily involved in the establishment of some
of these schools were "Black churches." For example, Wilber-
force and Shaw University in 1865, Morehouse in 1867, Bene-
dict in 1871, Rust in 1866, and Morgan State in 1867 all had
religious connections.

Also in the late 19th century and during the early 20th century (particularly following World War I) there began to be a
population shift of Blacks from the rural South to the urban
cities. This migration led to the establishment by Blacks of what
has come to be called "storefront churches." These were congregations housed in renovated stores. Such congregations had
a particular appeal to many Blacks who left the South looking
for familiar types of worship styles and not finding them in most
of the existing churches in the North.

In addition to storefront churches, other groups like the
"Black Muslims" and the Father Divine movement started to
flourish. There also began to be a steadily increasing professional
workforce and the development of national organizations other
than the church. Organizations such as the National Association for the Advancement of Colored People (NAACP) and the
Urban League evolved in the early part of the 20th century.

The 1950s and 1960s witnessed the influence of the "Black
Church" on and within the civil rights movement in a unique
way through the leadership of pastors and "ministers." Names
such as Adam Clayton Powell, Dr. Martin Luther King Jr.,
Ralph Abernathy, Leon Sullivan, and Jesse Jackson Sr. are
known to most. This was a natural connection because of the
high religious involvement of Blacks in general, the prominent

involvement of clergy in the civil rights movement, and the fact that "Black churches" were independent of White control. Hence these church settings provided a convenient place to rally and organize. Further, this connection was enhanced because the civil rights movement was rooted in the belief that discrimination and segregation are forms of injustice and, as such, are incompatible with the will of God. The civil rights movement also served as the basis for the increased emphasis on Black theology (see for example, Cone, 1970).

As the "Black Church" developed over time, there was carved out a powerful and unique role for the Black pastor. The Black pastor began to be perceived as, and was, a leader within both the local community and larger society. Historically, at least, the Black pastor was often the most educated and most articulate person within the community and was called upon to be its spokesperson. The role of the Black pastor will be discussed in detail in a later chapter.

THE LATTER HALF OF THE 20TH CENTURY AND THE EARLY 21ST CENTURY

Given this rich history, it should not be surprising that the wide influence of the "Black Church" has continued over time. For example, in a study by Taylor (1988), the correlates of religious noninvolvement among Black Americans were examined. Among his findings were:

- Only 8.2% of those surveyed reported that except for weddings and funerals they have never attended religious services as an adult
- 10.5% indicated that they had no current religious affiliation (younger persons, males, and non-Southerners were more likely to be non-affiliates)

- 40.9% of the respondents who had no religious affiliation and 48.2% of those who never attended religious services indicated that they pray every day
- 18% of the group indicated that they never prayed.

In a national representative cross-sectional survey of 2,107 Black adults, Taylor, Thornton, and Chatters (1987) found that 82.2% felt that the "Black Church" has helped the conditions of Blacks in America. Of that sample, 12.1% indicated that the church has made no difference, while only 4.9% indicated that it has hurt Blacks. Taylor, Chatters, and Levin (2004) reported that analyses from the National Study of Black Americans showed that fewer than 10% of Black Americans reported that they had not attended religious services as an adult except for weddings and funerals.

The "Black Church" was estimated in the early 1980s (see *Dollars and Sense*, 1981) to have ownership of 65,000 buildings at a value of 10.2 billion dollars. Approximately 1.7 billion dollars were being collected through plate offerings. Twenty million persons were estimated to be church members. The majority of the congregations at that time had incomes in the $10,000–$25,000 range. Approximately 67% of its membership was female.

Later sources obviously cite larger numbers. For example, Kunjufu (1994) gave the number of "Black congregations" at 75,000, while Malone (1994) estimated the total plate annual offering at approximately two billion dollars. These figures lend statistical support to the assertion that the "Black Church" continues to be the overall *single* most powerful force and institution within the Black community. While it has been suggested that the church has lost a portion of its grip on the Black community—which probably has some merit—as an institution, it must still be reckoned with if one is to significantly influence the

Black community politically, economically, psychologically, and most of all, spiritually.

As we now experience the early part of the 21st century, the "Black Church" is still the *single* most powerful institution for Blacks but now has more competing forces and several major challenges. A new phenomenon, the megachurch, is bursting on the scene. Furthermore, with the advent of cable television and the Internet, the "electronic church" is an issue with which one must deal. Nevertheless, the church continues with "a steady beat." There are also a rapidly increasing number of congregations; specifically, "Black churches," that are not part of the historical seven denominations formed after the Free African Society of 1787, as well as a seemingly increasing number of Blacks who are members of or are attending predominantly "White" congregations.

CONCLUSION

As we experience and observe the 21st century, there are "new" phenomena in the air. In popular culture, *Ebony* (2004) has described the changes as "The New Black Spirituality." These "new" phenomena and challenges to and within the "Black Church" and churches generally, if indeed they are new, must also be assessed and studied for their authenticity as well as impacts.

However, as we consider the history of Black people in the world, we have survived and thrived in spite of the odds. As the future unfolds and when that history is written, I believe that it will continue to show that as a group we are still a people of faith. Speaking futuristically, Williams and Dixie (2003) observed:

What will the stories be of black religious life of the twenty-first century? Will they simply follow the traditions of the past, or will they attempt to discover new vistas of faith? (p. 301).

Black Americans may choose one religious tradition over another—they may even invent new forms of worship—but they will always remain a people of faith . . . Only faith can inspire the dream of a better day. Faith and faith alone stands as a mighty sword to defend as well as a mighty arm of comfort and trumpet declaring to the world that this child, black, white, brown or any other color, is God's child. The story of black America is a story of faith fulfilled (pp. 302–303).

REFERENCES

Asante, M. (1988). *Afrocentricity.* Trenton: Africa World Press.

Bingham, D. J. (2002). *Pocket History of the Church.* Downers Grove: InterVarsity Press.

Cone, J. H. (1970). *Liberation: a Black Theology of Liberation.* Philadelphia: J. B. Lippincott.

Felder, C. H. (Editor) (1993). *Original African Heritage Study Bible—King James Version.* Nashville: James W. Winston Publishing.

Isichei, E. (1995). *A History of Christianity in Africa: from Antiquity to the Present.* Lawrenceville: Africa World Press.

June L. N. (1996). *African-American, Afrocentric (Africentric), Christian, and Male?* In June, L. N. and M. Parker (Editors) (1996). *Men to Men.* Grand Rapids: Zondervan.

King, M. L. Jr. (1998). *A Knock at Midnight.* In Carson, C. and P. Holloran (Editors). *A Knock at Midnight: Inspirations from the Great Sermons of Reverend Martin Luther King, Jr.* New York: Warner Books.

Kunjufu, J. (1994). *Adam! Where are You? Why Most Black Men Don't Go to Church.* Chicago: African American Images.

Lincoln, C. E. (1974). *The Black Church Since Frazier.* New York: Schocken Books.

Lincoln, C. E. and L. H. Mamiya (1990). *The Black Church in the African American Experience.* Durham: Duke University Press.

Low, A. L. and V. A. Clift (Editors) (1981). *Encyclopedia of Black America.* New York: McGraw-Hill.

Malone, W. Jr. (1994). *From Holy Power to Holy Profits: The Black Church and Community Economic Development.* Chicago: African American Images.

Mays, B. E. and J. W. Nicholson (1933). *The Negro's Church.* New York: New York Universities Press.

Mbiti, J. S. (1970). *African Religions and Philosophy.* Garden City: Anchor Books.

_____ (1975). *Introduction to African Religion.* Portsmouth: Heinemann.

McCray, W. A. (1990a). *The Black Presence in the Bible: Discovering the Black and African Identity of Biblical Persons and Nations.* Volume 1. Chicago: Black Light Fellowship.

_____ (1990b). *The Black Presence in the Bible and the Table of Nations—Genesis 10:1–32.* Volume 2. Chicago: Black Light Fellowship.

Raboteau, A. J. (1980). *Slave Religion—The "Invisible Institution" in the Antebellum South.* New York: Oxford University Press.

_____ (2001). *Canaan Land: A Religious History of African Americans.* New York: Oxford.

Taylor, R. J. (1988). "Correlates of Religious Non-Involvement Among Black Americans." *Review of Religious Research,* 29, 126–139.

Taylor, R. J., M. C. Thornton, and L. M. Chatters (1987). "Black Americans' Perceptions of the Sociohistorical Role of the Church." *Journal of Black Studies,* 18, 123–38.

Taylor, R. J., L. M. Chatters, and J. Levin (2004). *Religion in the Lives of African Americans—Social, Psychological, and Health Perspectives.* Thousands Oaks: Sage Publications.

"The Black Church in America." (1981). *Dollars and Sense Magazine* (Special Issue).

"The New Black Spirituality." (December, 2004). *Ebony.* Chicago: Johnson Publishing.

"The Search for Adam and Eve." (January 11, 1988). *Newsweek* Magazine.

Turner, V. S. Sr. (1999). *A History of African American Evangelistic Activity.* In June, L. N. and M. Parker (Editors). *Evangelism and Discipleship in African American Churches.* Grand Rapids: Zondervan.

Walker, W. T. (1979). *Somebody's Calling My Name: Black Sacred Music and Social Change.* Valley Forge: Judson Press.

Williams, C. (1976). *The Destruction of Black Civilization: Great Issues of a Race from 4500 B.C. to 2000 A.D.* Chicago: Third World Press.

Williams, J. and Q. Dixie (2003). *This Far by Faith.* New York: Amistad—An Imprint of Harper-Collins.

Wilmore, G. S. (1973). *Black Religion and Black Radicalism: an Examination of the Black Experience in Religion.* Garden City: Anchor.

Woodson, C. G. (1921). *The History of the Negro Church.* Washington, D.C.: Associated Publishers.

_____ (1933). *The Mis-education of the Negro.* Washington, D.C.: Associated Publishers.

CHAPTER 2

A Review of
Psychology and Religion—
Western and African Styles

*"And God blessed them, and God said unto them, Be
fruitful, and multiply, and replenish the earth, and
subdue it: and have dominion over the fish of the sea,
and over the fowl of the air, and over every living
thing that moveth upon the earth."*

GENESIS 1:28

INTRODUCTION

BASIC ELEMENTS OF PSYCHOLOGY

Because the purpose of this book is to take a look at the church through psychological and biblical, or spiritual lenses, it is important to now examine the goals, purposes, and limitations of psychology. Both the goals and purposes of psychology have evolved over the years.

In general usage, psychology is defined in *The American Heritage Dictionary—Fourth Edition* (2004) as: (1) "the science that deals with mental processes and behavior; and (2) the emotional and behavioral characteristics of an individual, a group, or an activity" (p. 1125). According to Kalat (2005) in the book *Introduction to Psychology*, the term "psychology is derived from the Greek roots *psyche*, meaning 'soul' or 'mind,' and *logos*, meaning 'word.' In the late 1800s and early 1900s psychology was defined as the scientific study of the mind" (p. 3). However, according to Kalat (2005), psychologists became dissatisfied with this definition and redefined the term as the study of behavior. For the early part of the 21st century, Kalat defines psychology as the "systematic study of behavior and experience" (p. 3). In *The APA Dictionary of Psychology* (VandenBos, 2007), psychology is defined as "the study of the mind and behavior" (p. 753). The definition given by VandenBos continues by stating that:

The practice of psychology involves the use of psychological knowledge for any of several purposes: to understand and treat mental, emotional, physical, and psychological dysfunction; to understand and enhance behavior in various settings of human activity . . . ; and to improve machine and building design for human use" (p. 753).

These definitions are primarily European or Western definitions. Furthermore, Western or European psychology as a distinct and recognized field is relatively new in comparison to other sciences.

The popularity of psychology increased tremendously during the 20th century. In Christian circles, however, psychology has been both embraced and viewed with disdain. Within the "Black Church," psychology is still viewed with suspicion and caution, though there was greater acceptance of it in the last quarter of the 20th century, which has continued into the early part of the 21st century.

The elements that comprise or make up psychology are as old as civilization itself. In the writings of the Egyptians and Greeks, rudiments of what may be described as psychology are seen (Kambon, 1998; Akbar, 2004a). The basic fundamentals and foci of psychology are numerous and depend upon the branch of psychology one is studying and the issues with which one is dealing: clinical, counseling, experimental, physiological, industrial, etc.

The common or core elements across the various branches of psychology are found in its definition as an attempt to define, describe, understand, and influence behavior. Therefore, psychology (particularly Western psychology) attempts to determine causes of behavior, what maintains behavior, how to change behaviors, how actions and experiences affect the body, the emotional and behavioral characteristics of individuals, groups, or activities, etc.

WESTERN PSYCHOLOGY AND RELIGION

There has often been a strained relationship between psychology (as well as psychiatry) and religion, particularly Christianity (Adams, 1970; Kelsey, 1986; Mowrer, 1961; and Vitz, 1977). Numerous psychologists, psychiatrists, and psychoanalysts have examined the topic of religion and have had various views (positive and negative) on the subject. Below, some of these views of the earlier writers will be discussed.

Sigmund Freud. Sigmund Freud, for example, dealt with religion in such books as: *The Future of an Illusion* (1964; originally published in 1927), *Totem and Taboo* (1950; originally published in 1916), and *Moses and Monotheism* (1939). Freud attempted to explain the origin of religion and the psychological role it plays in one's life. Needless to say, within Christian circles, Freud's books, though considered classics in the broader educational arena, are not held in high esteem in terms of objective and adequate explanations of religion.

The essence of Freud's thesis is that religion is a phenomenon created by individuals to help them deal with their neuroticism and sense of finiteness. In the book *The Future of an Illusion,* he said:

> I have tried to show that religious ideas have arisen from the same need as have all achievements of civilization: from the necessity of defending oneself against the crushing force of nature. To this a second motive was added—the urge to rectify the shortcomings of civilization which made themselves painfully felt (p. 30).

Religious ideas are teachings and assertions about facts and conditions of external (or internal) reality which tell one something one has not discovered for oneself and which lay claim to one's belief (p. 37).

I think we have prepared the way sufficiently for an answer to both these questions. It will be found if we turn our attention to the psychical origin of religious ideas. These, which are given out as teachings, are not precipitates of experience or end-results of thinking: they are illusions, fulfillments of the oldest, strongest and most urgent wishes of mankind. The secret of their strength lies in the strength of those wishes . . . Thus the benevolent rule of a divine Providence allays our fear of the dangers of life . . . (p. 47).

An illusion is not the same as an error; nor is it necessarily an error . . . What is characteristic of illusions is that they are derived from human wishes . . . Illusions need not necessarily be false—that is to say, unrealizable or in contradiction to reality . . . Thus we call a belief an illusion when a wish-fulfillment is a prominent factor in its motivation, and in doing so we disregard its relations to reality, just as the illusion itself sets no store by verification (pp. 48–49).

Though Freud continues to be a very popular figure, his works, per se, have not had much influence in the area of "Black religious thought."

Eric Fromm. Fromm discussed the subject of psychology and religion in books such as *Psychoanalysis and Religion* (1967) and *The Art of Loving* (1963). His treatise of religion within Christian circles is regarded somewhat in the same vein as Freud. Though his book, *The Art of Loving*, presents a detailed analysis of love from a humanistic perspective, it falls short of embracing or exploring the biblical aspects of love. For example, in this book Fromm stated:

> Having spoken of the love of God, I want to make it clear that I myself do not think in terms of a theistic concept, and that to me the concept of God is only a historically conditioned one, in which man has expressed his experience of his higher powers, his longing for truth and for unity at a given historical period. But I believe also that the consequences of strict monotheism and a non-theistic ultimate concern with the spiritual reality are two views, which, though different, need not fight each other (pp. 60–61).

Other Early Western Psychologists. Other treatises of the psychology of religion are done somewhat more positively. For example, Gordon Allport: *The Individual and His Religion* (1950); William James: *The Varieties of Religious Experience* (1958; lectures delivered in 1901–1902); Carl Jung: *Modern Man in Search of a Soul* (1933) and *Answer to Job* (1960); and Abraham Maslow: *Religions, Values, and Peak-Experiences* (1970); are all considered Western or European classics. Another significant work in the area of psychology and religion is Franz Delitzsch's: *A System of Biblical Psychology* (1966; originally published in 1899).

TWENTIETH-CENTURY WESTERN PSYCHOLOGY

Most of the books mentioned above were first published in the early to middle 20th century. The middle of the 20th century saw a lull in terms of psychology and religion but there has been a resurgence of interest. In the latter half of the 20th century, for example, attempts at the integration of psychology and religion/Christianity were made. Conferences were held throughout the country and several articles and books were written. Representative of early works in this area of integration are Donaldson: *Research in Mental Health and Religious Behavior: An Introduction to Research in the Integration of Christianity and the Behavioral Sciences* (1976); Carter and Narramore: *The Integration of Psychology and Theology* (1979); Vitz: *Psychology as Religion* (1977); Kelsey: *Christianity as Psychology* (1986); and Crabb: *Basic Principles of Biblical Counseling* (1975). These books, written by authors who profess to be Christians, demonstrate the renewed interest in this topic by the broader church community during the latter half of the 20th century. They have helped fuel the interest that continues today.

ELEMENTS OF A WESTERN
PSYCHOLOGY OF RELIGION—DEFINITIONS

What makes for a definition of a psychology of religion, a psychology of Christianity, or a biblical psychology? Delitzsch (1966) stated, "Biblical psychology is no science of yesterday. It is one of the oldest sciences of the church" (p. 3). He defined biblical psychology as a "scientific representation of the doctrine of Scripture on the psychical constitution of man as it was created, and the ways in which this constitution has been affected by sin and redemption" (p. 16).

Allport (1950) in the book *The Individual and His Religion* states that:

A man's religion is the audacious bid he makes to bind himself to creation and to the Creator. It is his ultimate attempt to enlarge and to complete his own personality by finding the supreme context in which he rightly belongs (p. 161).

William James (1958) in *The Varieties of Religious Experience* defined religion as: "The feelings, acts, and experiences of individual men in their solitude, so far as they apprehend themselves to stand in relation to whatever they may consider the divine" (p. 42).

Meadow and Kahoe (1984) in the book *Psychology of Religion* state that:

> . . . because we are able to think, to reflect on our predicaments and destinies, much of the insecurities of human life originates in the mind, the psyche of the person. Thus security and a number of other human needs are considered psychological in origin, or *psychogenic* (p. 20).

The other needs beyond security that Meadow and Kahoe list that are considered psychogenic are: relationship, adventure, power, and status.

Kelsey (1986) in the book *Christianity as Psychology* made the observation that:

> The religious community needs to integrate the knowledge of depth psychology into its view of human beings so that the understandings of the depth and complexity of our psyches and how we develop by stages into mature human beings is available to ministers and lay people (p. 112).

Thus writers who profess to be of the Christian faith have also stressed the importance of psychology and psychological principles in the lives of Christians.

A Focus on the
Psychology of Religion—African Style

This section will give a brief history of Black psychology, present the definitions of Black psychology; discuss the elements covered in Black psychology, and present Black psychology's viewpoints on religion and Christianity.

History of Black Psychology

During the 1960s, corresponding with the civil rights movement, there was a resurgence of interest in articulating a field of study called Black or African Psychology. This resurgence followed shortly after the formation of the Association of Black Psychologists in 1968. Joseph White (1970) in an article called this movement: "Toward a Black Psychology." This article, first published in *Ebony* magazine, was a significant work in that it followed the 1960s when "revolutionary" thinking resurged in the African American community. While White's article did not contain a precise definition, its main contribution was in pointing out the limitations of Western psychology and the need for an alternative conceptual approach, particularly in regard to persons of African descent.

The work of Wade Nobles (1986) is very informative in an understanding of the history of the Black psychology movement. He aptly noted that different writers put the date of the inception of Black or African psychology at different points depending upon historical reference points. Nobles (1986) stated that "the inception of Black Psychology is somewhat clouded" (p. 63). For Nobles, four reference points are possible:

1) The awarding of Frances Sumner's degree in 1920 from Clark University in Massachusetts. Sumner was the first Black person to receive a Ph.D. in psychology.

2) The formation of the Association of Black Psychologists. This organization came into being in 1968, in part, as a reaction to the American Psychological Association's failure to address the needs of Blacks adequately. Dr. Charles Thomas was the Association's first president.

3) The reactive phase of Black psychology. Using this as a marker would date the origin to the 1970s.

4) The era in Ancient Egypt (Kmt) when Blacks were pondering the issue of human behavior. With this as a marker, Black psychology is more than 4,000 years old.

Those interested in more details regarding the origin of Black psychology are encouraged to read White (1970), Nobles (1986, particularly chapters 1 and 5), Guthrie (2004), Kambon (1998), and Akbar (2004a).

I believe that it is more appropriate to place the origin of Black psychology in ancient Africa. What happened in the 20th century was the sowing of the proper seeds for a resurgence of attention to this area.

Definition of Black Psychology and the Areas Covered

Nobles (1986) gave the following definitions of Black Psychology:

The study of the human spirit or the study of human illumination (understanding) (p. 1).

The study of the soul belonging to a particular group of people whose class membership is rooted in the historical and cultural experience of African people and who are euphemistically called Black (p. 47).

The discipline charged with understanding the fundamental nature of human beings. It is a process of "returning to the source" while groping toward the future (p. 107).

Kambon (1998) defines Black psychology as: "a system of knowledge/philosophy, definitions, concepts, models, procedures and practice regarding the nature of the social universe from the perspective of African Cosmology/the African Worldview" (p. 525). By cosmology, Kambon means "the system for organizing, experiencing, constructing, and describing the structure of reality, the cosmos, the Universe, that is indigenous to a racial cultural group. It represents the ideational and philosophical underpinnings of culture" (p. 528).

Thus African cosmology then is cosmology from an African perspective. For Kambon, an African worldview is:

> . . . the conceptual-ideological framework derived from African Cosmology which projects African reality, history, culture, philosophy (ontology, axiology, epistemology-science, etc.) as the center of the universe. It represents the African survival thrust of spiritualism, collectivism-interconnectedness, and harmony with Nature, inherent in African Cosmology (p. 527).

Regarding psychology and its definition, Akbar (2004b) stated:

> Psychology is a Greek word revealing its most recent origins among the Greek students of the Ancient African masters as "Psyche" frequently identified with a Greek goddess of the same name actually means "soul." According to Massey (1974), the word *psyche* is actually derived from the Egyptian in which *khe* is the soul and *su* is she: hence the feminine nature of the Greek *psu-khe*. Without the article "P," *sakhu*

means the "understanding, the illuminator, the eye and the soul of being; that which inspires." Not only is the study of the mind derived from ancient Egypt, but even the word used to characterize that study is of Kemitic origin (p. 200).

Akbar (2004a) further states that Black or African psychology "maintains that the essence of the human being is spiritual" (p. 35).

What is clear in the various definitions of Black psychology is that Black psychology roots itself in the history of a people and out of this history comes the discipline. Black psychology is more than the study of observable behaviors and as a discipline deals with the psyche (soul) in its truest sense. Thus Black psychology, in contrast to Western or European psychology, has always been more open to the spiritual side of humans. However, as noted earlier, in the latter part of the 20th century, Western psychology became again more open to the spiritual.

To understand how European and Black psychology diverge, one must consider the traditional European and African/Black worldviews. Black psychology's schematic in contrast to the European is described in Table 1 on the following page. According to Kambon (1998) the differences are as follow:

Table I
COMPARATIVE WORLDVIEWS SCHEMATIC
Source: Kambon, K. K. K. (1998); page 130, Table 3.2
(Used by verbal permission—5/23/2007)

European/European-American Worldview	African/African-American Worldview
Ethos	
Control/Mastery over Nature	Oneness/Harmony with Nature
Survival of the Fittest	Survival of the Group
Values & Customs	
Exclusiveness/Dichotomy	Inclusiveness/Synthesis
Competition-Individual Rights	Cooperation-Collective Responsibility
Separateness-Independence	Corporateness and Interdependence
Materialism-Ordinality	Spiritualism-Circularity
Intervention-Oppression and Aggression	Complimentarity-Understanding
Psycho-Behavioral Modality	
Individualism	Groupness
Uniqueness-Differences	Sameness-Commonality
European/White Supremacy (Racism/Anti-African)	Humanism-Religious

Further, Black psychology is strength-based as opposed to deficit-oriented. Critical to Black psychology is the concept of the Maafa. According to Kambon (1998), Maafa is:

a 'Kiswahilli' term meaning more or less a (prolonged) period of great disaster. It usually refers to The African Holocaust of Eurasian-European enslavement beginning in Africa under the Arabs and continuing through the so called Western Europeans. It also sometimes refers to the approximately 2,500–3,000

years of continuous violent encroachment upon African civi-
lization/African reality by Eurasians-Europeans beginning in
Kemet (such as around 500 BCE or even earlier during the
Hyksos invasion) and extending into the present (p. 530).

Because of the Maafa, a goal of Black psychology is to help
restore the Ma'at. The Ma'at "refers to cosmic order and balance as the cardinal principles governing the dynamic functioning of all aspects at all levels of the universe" (Kambon,
1998, p. 44). Grills (2004) believes that African psychology
covers several fundamental concepts. These are: worldview and
its metaphysical basis of psychology and African science, concepts of consciousness, conceptualizations of the person and
human beingness, concepts of health and illness, and models of
the healing exchange or process.

Thus the areas covered in Black psychology are delineated
in its definitions. Hence, Black psychology in its truest sense
does not compartmentalize humans into body, mind, and spirit,
but rather sees a clear connection and continuity among the
three. Black psychology, likewise, deals with behaviors, experiences, and emotions while it respects the need to openly engage the "spiritual." It also promotes the belief that humans are
spiritual beings and in order to be "healthy," behaviors must
be in line with the "spiritual."

Black Psychology and its Relation to Religion

As can be concluded from the preceding section, Black psychology is closely linked to religion and the spiritual. Black psychologists (its theorists) are very comfortable using the idea of
"spiritual" and the "divine." Black psychology sees human beings as "spiritual" in the broad sense of the concept and therefore is interested in exploring this aspect of humanity.
Spirituality (Kambon, 1998) is defined as "the vital (invisible,

dynamic) life force in African reality, which defines its essence and functions to bond-connect everything in existence. Rhythm is seen as its synthesizing-interconnecting manifestation" (p. 532).

I find that the overall contributions of Black psychology are critical to an understanding of African people. However, while I appreciate the general field of Black psychology's greater openness—from its inception, to the spiritual—some writers in this area do not have a positive view of Christianity. It is on this point that I part company with some of its theorists and writers.

This discontent and sometimes rejection of Christianity by some of the writers and practitioners of Black psychology is often because Christianity as well as other religions is seen as a part of and a major contributor to the Maafa. My own belief is that we must accept the fact that throughout history Christianity has been marred and deeply stained where there has been participation in and often defense of the oppression of Black people. However, in such cases, that has been an aberrant form of Christianity. A thorough look at Christianity will reveal such. For, as was pointed out in chapter one, Christianity in its original form can also be considered traditional to African people and in its true form is appropriate for African people today.

Making Use of the Best of Western and African Psychology

Therefore, given the caveats and cautions mentioned above, and armed with both the best of the tools of African/Black and Western psychology, I will in the remaining chapters delve into the essential purpose of this book. That is, to explore how psychology has exhibited itself in the lives of peoples of African descent through the church and how we have dealt with our situation on the world stage. The primary goal of this book is to look at the positive and the negative aspects of our Christian religious experiences through psychological and biblical (spiritual) lenses with an ultimate aim of suggesting how Christianity can be lived and practiced more effectively in the years ahead by all communities of faith.

Hence the psychological treatment of Christianity, which is this book's primary focus, will deal with our individual and collective feelings, emotions, struggles, activities, experiences, and behaviors in reference to God, Jesus Christ, and the Holy Spirit as exemplified in and through the Christian community with a special focus on the "Black Church." Such a treatment will deal with the values and benefits one derives from religious involvement. It will also deal with what develops the religious behavior as well as what maintains it.

Thus, by definition, there is a psychology of and in religion and more specifically there is a psychology of and in Christianity. Making such a claim does not imply that psychology is Christianity or that Christianity is psychology. Rather it suggests that Christianity (religion and the church) can be looked at from a psychological perspective while preserving its essence. Indeed, human beings who embrace Christianity are mind, body, soul, and spirit. As such, because the mind, behaviors, and soul are involved, so is psychology.

CONCLUSION

Psychology provides a valuable tool for observing and understanding various aspects of human beings. This tool will be put to work in the chapters that follow.

REFERENCES

Adams, J. E. (1970). *Competent to Counsel*. Grand Rapids: Baker Book House.

Akbar, N. (2004a). *The Evolution of Human Psychology for African Americans*. In Jones, R. L. (Editor). *Black Psychology* (Fourth Edition). Hampton: Cobb & Henry.

_____ (2004b). *Akbar Papers in African Psychology*. Tallahassee: Mind Productions.

Allport, G. W. (1950). *The Individual and His Religion*. New York: MacMillan.

Carter, J. D. and B. Narramore (1979). *The Integration of Psychology and Theology: An Introduction*. Grand Rapids: Zondervan.

Crabb, L. Jr. (1975). *Basic Principles of Biblical Counseling*. Grand Rapids: Zondervan.

Delitzsch, F. (1966; originally published 1899). *A System of Biblical Psychology*. Grand Rapids: Baker Book House.

Donaldson, W. J. Jr. (Editor) (1976). *Research in Mental Health and Religious Behavior: An Introduction to Research in the Integration of Christianity and the Behavioral Sciences*. Atlanta: The Psychological Studies Institute, Inc.

Freud, S. (1964). *The Future of an Illusion*. Garden City: Anchor Books.

_____ (1939). *Moses and Monotheism*. New York: Vintage Books.

_____ (1950). *Totem and Taboo*. New York: W.W. Norton.

Fromm, E. (1963). *The Art of Loving*. New York: Bantam Books.

_____ (1967). *Psychoanalysis and Religion*. New York: Bantam Books.

Grills, C. T. (2004). *African Psychology*. In Jones, R. L. (Editor). *Black Psychology* (Fourth Edition). Hampton: Cobb & Henry.

Guthrie, R. V. (2004). *The Psychology of African Americans: An Historical Perspective*. In Jones, R. L. (Editor). *Black Psychology* (Fourth Edition). Hampton: Cobb & Henry.

James, W. (1958). *The Varieties of Religious Experience*. New York: Mentor.

Jung, C. J. (1933). *Modern Man in Search of a Soul*. New York: Harvest.

_____ (1960). *Answer to Job—The Problem of Evil: Its Psychological and Religious Origins*. Cleveland: Meridan.

Kalat, J. W. (2005). *Introduction to Psychology* (7th Edition). Belmont, CA: Thomson Wadsworth.

Kambon, K. K. (1998). *African/Black Psychology in the American Context—An African-Centered Approach*. Tallahassee: Nubian Nation.

Kelsey, M. (1986). *Christianity as Psychology: The Healing Power of the Christian Message*. Minneapolis: Augsburg.

Maslow, A. H. (1970). *Religions, Values, and Peak-Experiences*. New York: The Viking Press.

Meadow, M. J. and R. D. Kahoe (1984). *Psychology of Religion: Religion in Individual Lives*. New York: Harper and Row.

Mowrer, O. H. (1961). *The Crisis in Psychiatry and Religion*. New York: D. Van Nostrand.

Nobles, W. W. (1986). *African Psychology—Toward its Reclamation, Reascension and Revitalization.* Oakland: A Black Family Publication.

The American Heritage College Dictionary (Fourth Edition) (2004). New York: Houghton Mifflin.

VandenBos, G. R. (2007) (Editor in Chief). *APA Dictionary of Psychology.* Washington, D.C.: American Psychological Association.

Vitz, P. C. (1977). *Psychology as Religion—The Cult of Self Worship.* Grand Rapids: Eerdmans.

White, J. L. "Toward a Black Psychology." (1970, September). *Ebony,* 25, 44–45, 48–50, 52.

PART 2
TYPOLOGIES, MODELS, AND NAMES

Types and Models of Churches

■

Types of Members

CHAPTER 3

Types and Models of Churches

"Know ye not that ye are the temple of God, and that the Spirit of God dwelleth in you?"

1 CORINTHIANS 3:16

"Unto the angel of the church of Ephesus write . . ."

REVELATION 2:1

"And I say also unto thee, That thou art Peter, and upon this rock I will build my church; and the gates of hell shall not prevail against it."

MATTHEW 16:18

INTRODUCTION

Various characterizations of churches have been advanced in both the literature on Christianity and religion, as well as in popular culture. These characterizations are summarized and presented here because they provide information of which one should be aware. One should also attend to these distinctions primarily because they represent the views held both by some within and outside of the religious community. In presenting them, I am not necessarily endorsing them. However, I believe that a review and discussion of some of these characterizations will aid in understanding the views held, the possible needs served, the issues involved, and the potential appeal of the various church types and settings to individuals and situations over time. In considering these types, it should be remembered that some of these characterizations have not been empirically examined.

The church types to be reviewed and discussed are presented in Table 2. Following the discussion of the church types, there will be a review and discussion of church models. Models give more detailed and complete analyses of churches than do types.

Table 2
VARIOUS CHURCH TYPES

Book of Revelation	Lincoln & Mamiya	Kunjufu	Martin Luther King Jr.	Gibbs	Barna/Barna & Jackson	Warren	Other General Descriptions
Ephesus	African Methodist Episcopal	Entertainment	Freeze-up	Missional	Highly effective	Purpose Driven	Storefront Church
Smyrna	African Methodist Episcopal Zion	Containment	Burn-up			Soul Winning	Megachurch Breakout (see Rainer, 2005)
Pergamos	Christian Methodist Episcopal	Liberation	Fresh Bread		High impact	Experience God	
Thyatira							
Sardis	National Baptist Convention, USA, Incorporated					Family Reunion	Connecting Church and the Serving Church
Philadelphia						Classroom	Classroom Church (see Malphurs, 2007)
Laodicea	National Baptist Convention of America, Unincorporated					Socially Conscious	
	Progressive National Baptist Convention						
	Church of God in Christ						

In the book of Revelation, chapters one to three, Jesus Christ speaks to the apostle John and describes seven church types (local assemblies) which John then wrote about. These are called by the names Ephesus, Smyrna, Pergamos, Thyatira, Sardis, Philadelphia, and Laodicea. Below are their descriptions as given in the book of Revelation.

The Church at Ephesus:
- It is known by its works; its labor and patience.
- It cannot bear (tolerate) those who are evil.
- It has tested those who said they were apostles and were not and found them to be liars.
- It labors for Christ's sake and has not fainted.
- It is challenged to repent and do the first works.
- It hates the work of the Nicolaitans.

The Church at Smyrna:
- Its works, tribulation, and poverty are known by Christ.
- Some of its members will suffer; they will be cast into prison in order to be tried and will have tribulation.
- It is encouraged to be faithful unto death.

The Church at Pergamos:
- Its works are known.
- It has held fast to the name of Christ and has not denied faith in Him.
- It has among them those that hold to the doctrine of the Nicolaitans, a doctrine which Christ hates.
- They are admonished to repent.

The Church at Thyatira:
- Its works, love, service, and patience are known.
- It allows Jezebel, the one that called herself a prophetess, to teach and to seduce Christ's servants to commit fornication and to eat things sacrificed unto idols.
- Jezebel was given time to repent of her fornication and she did not. If she and those that commit adultery with her do not repent, they will be destroyed.
- It is told to hold fast until Christ returns.
- If it holds on, it will be given power.

The Church at Sardis:
- Its works are known.
- It has a name that says they live but are dead.
- It is told to be watchful and strengthen the things that remain.
- Its works have not been found to be perfect.
- It is admonished to hold fast and to repent.
- If it is not watchful, Christ will come unto them as a thief in the night.

The Church at Philadelphia:
- Its works are known.
- It has a little strength, has kept Christ's Word, and has not denied His name.
- It has kept the word of Christ's patience and thus will be kept from the hour of temptation which will come to try (test) those on earth.
- They are admonished to hold fast.
- For those who overcome, they will be rewarded.

The Church at Laodicea:
- Their works are known.

- They are neither hot or cold and are criticized for being such.
- Since they are lukewarm (neither hot or cold), Christ will spew them out of His mouth.
- It says it is rich and increased in goods, and has no need of anything.
- It does not know that it is wretched, miserable, poor, blind, and naked.
- Because of their actual state, they are counseled to buy of Christ gold tried in fire so that they can be rich, clothed, not naked, and can see.
- They are admonished to repent of apostasy.

These churches in the book of Revelation are presented to show that church "types" are represented in the Scriptures.

LINCOLN AND MAMIYA'S TYPOLOGY

In the book *The Black Church in the African American Experience,* Lincoln and Mamiya (1990) describe the seven historical Black denominations as: "those independent, historic, and totally black controlled denominations, which were founded after the Free African Society of 1787 and which constituted the core of black Christians" (p. 1). As already referenced in the Introduction, the seven denominations (typologies) included under this definition are:

- African Methodist Episcopal (A.M.E.)
- African Methodist Episcopal Zion (A.M.E.Z.)
- Christian Methodist Episcopal (C.M.E.)
- National Baptist Convention, U.S.A., Incorporated (NBC)

- National Baptist Convention of America, Unincorporated (NBCA)
- Progressive National Baptist Convention (PNBC)
- Church of God in Christ (COGIC)

Lincoln and Mamiya's description is not a typology in the general sense of the word; rather, the description has its usefulness because it is a shorthand way of describing what has come to be known as the traditional "Black Church" and represent in the general sense what are known as denominations. Hence, no psychological interpretation of these denominations will be attempted.

KUNJUFU'S TYPOLOGIES

Writing, more or less, in the popular and nonempirical vein, in the book *Adam! Where are You!* Kunjufu (1994) describes three church types (he calls them categories): the entertainment, the containment, and the liberation. The entertainment church as described by Kunjufu (1994) is:

> a church where there is a lot of whooping, hollering and singing, to the exclusion of teaching and working. It is a church that makes you feel good for the moment but does not address societal issues. The church administrators may have activities during the week but they do not empower the congregation culturally, politically, or economically (p. 23).

Using Kunjufu's characterization, an entertainment church focuses on giving short-term comfort and support to those who attend and has little or no interest in the broader societal issues. Such a church type is mostly interested in the attendees shouting and "feeling good" during the time that the congregants are together.

The entertainment church type is most likely to appeal to those who see the worship service mainly as a means of "catharsis" (the releasing of pent-up feelings) and those who believe that shouting and outward expressions of emotions are the primary needs and goals of the attendees. This church type may become, for some (unconsciously so), a substitute or extension of the former secular dance hall. Such a church type is probably maintained by a pastor who, in the language of the apostle Paul, is providing "milk" rather than "meat" to the congregation (1 Corinthians 3:2).

Kunjufu defines the containment churches as: "very similar to entertainment churches except that they are open only from 11:00 a.m.–1:00 p.m. on Sundays and are closed the remainder of the week" (p. 23). The containment church has some of the elements of the entertainment church but is noted by its primary emphasis on issues dealing with its own survival and its doors are open only for worship services. Hence, no activities are provided for its members beyond the Sunday worship service time. The containment church is most likely to appeal to those who do not have a complete vision or broad understanding of the role of the biblical church. Similar to the entertainment church, the teaching and leadership in this type of congregation do not lead the worshipers to see Christianity and Christ in their fullness.

Finally, Kunjufu defines the liberation church as:

the church in which Nat Turner, Harriet Tubman, Denmark Vesey, Sojourner Truth, Gabriel Prosser, Richard Allen, Ida B. Wells, and Marcus Garvey were members. This church understands the liberation theology of Luke 4:18–20: "The Lord has appointed me to preach the Gospel to the poor and heal the brokenhearted." It is based on the liberation theology of Isaiah 58, where we must feed the hungry and clothe the naked; and

67

James 2:26 which helps us to understand that the cross is both vertical and horizontal: without the spirit our labor is in vain, and work without faith is dead (p. 23).

The liberation church type is one in which its members are taught the Word of God with an emphasis on growth and development so that they can live a more complete life in Christ in such a manner that they are set free. "Black churches" that fit this mold will emphasize their cultural/African heritage, make sure that their members are well versed in history, and will be appropriately politically involved. The liberation "Black Church" will likely attract those who have a deeper knowledge of history of Black peoples in the Diaspora, are more Afrocentric in their worldviews, and are possibly more mature spiritually.

DR. MARTIN LUTHER KING JR.'S TYPOLOGY

As one reads the writings and listens to the speeches of Dr. Martin Luther King Jr., one encounters an individual who loved and was deeply involved and committed to the institutional church. Overall, he saw the institutional church as a positive factor in the lives of Christians, yet on many occasions he was critical of both the "White Church" and the "Black Church" communities on certain dimensions. He did this because he wanted the institutional church to be better.

Three church types are given by Dr. Martin Luther King Jr. in the sermon "A Knock at Midnight" (see Carson and Holloran, 1998). These, like the Kunjufu categories, are not empirically based. Two types of churches are explicitly referenced and a third can be gleaned from a careful examination of this sermon. As in the case of Kunjufu, two of these types are viewed negatively and one is viewed positively.

The first type, the "Freeze-Up Church," has the following characteristics, according to King:

- It considers itself a dignified church.
- It brags on its members by telling how many lawyers, doctors, schoolteachers, and businesspeople it has.
- The pastor preaches an essay on Sunday mornings. The pastor is afraid to really preach a sermon and say it with passion and conviction.
- The choir does not sing gospel songs.
- It is ashamed of its heritage.
- The members are ashamed that they are Black and that their ancestral home is Africa.

The second type, the "Burn-Up Church," has the following characteristics:

- The pastor does not prepare any sermon. Rather than preparing a sermon, the pastor relies on volume (referring to the voice level) rather than content.
- There is more religion in the members' hands and feet than in their heart and soul.
- This church has zeal of God, but not according to knowledge.
- The members leave the service on Sunday morning and if one asks a member what the pastor preached about, the member would say, "I don't know but he preached this morning."

The third type, not explicitly stated, is what I will label the "Fresh Bread Church." It is labeled this way because in the latter part of the sermon, after describing the "freeze-up" and "burn-up" church types, King challenges the church to keep the bread fresh. By "bread," he means the Gospel, the Word of God. He does this after saying that the church has the bread of life. Thus this church would have the following characteristics:

- The message (bread) is kept fresh (it is relevant to the issues the members are currently facing).
- It has the bread of life.
- If a young or an old person would come by this church seeking answers to life's problems, the church could help.
- If a person is caught up in sexual promiscuity, this church could help.

A transcription of this sermon is found in the edited book by Carson and Holloran (1998). When one consults this book, one will note some discrepancies between the taped sermon and the transcriptions. I chose for this book to use the words from the audio version of the taped sermon because it is slightly more detailed (Carson and Holloran, 1998).

As to who might be attracted to these churches considering the King typology, for the "freeze-up" and "burn-up" churches, the attraction would be similar to what has been indicated for Kunjufu's entertainment and containment churches. Likewise, King's "fresh bread" church type would be similar to what has been stated for Kunjufu's liberation church.

GIBBS' TYPOLOGY

Gibbs (2000) describes what he calls a "missional" church, which is defined as one that "draws attention to the essential nature and vocation of the church as God's called and sent people" (p. 51). He defines "mission" to indicate the action of sending and views it as the central theme describing the purpose of God's action in human history. Gibbs cites twelve empirical indicators of a missional church (p. 52):

- It proclaims the Gospel [this is evangelism].
- It is a community where all members are involved in learning to become disciples of Jesus [this is discipleship].
- The Bible is normative in the life of the church.
- The church understands itself as different from the world because of its participation in the life, death, and resurrection of the Lord.
- The church seeks to discern God's specific missional vocation for the entire community and for all its members.
- Christians behave in a Christianly manner toward one another.
- The church is a community that practices reconciliation.
- People within the community hold themselves accountable to one another in love.
- The church practices hospitality.
- Worship is the central act by which the community celebrates with joy and thanksgiving for both God's presence and God's promised future.
- The church is a community that has a vital public witness.
- There is recognition that the church itself is an incomplete expression of the reign of God.

The missional church is similar to King's "fresh bread" church and Kunjufu's liberation church and the attractiveness of this church type would be the same as already described. These church types focus on helping individuals to live mature Christian lives with a proper balance of this world and the world to come.

71

BARNA'S TYPOLOGIES

George Barna and his associates have been conducting re-search on religious behaviors and trends for a number of years. This research has resulted in at least two descriptions of churches: the "highly effective church" and "high impact churches." As to "highly effective churches," nine character-istics or habits are identified in the book *The Habits of Highly Effective Churches* (Barna, 1999). These congregations:

- rely upon strategic leadership
- organize to facilitate highly effective ministry
- emphasize developing significant relationships within the congregation
- help congregants invest themselves in genuine worship
- engage in strategic evangelism
- get people involved in systematic theological growth
- utilize holistic stewardship practices
- serve the needy people in the community
- equip families to minister to themselves (p. 24).

The above characteristics, which are probably applicable to congregations regardless of ethnicity, are abstracted from sur-veying primarily White congregations. Barna's (1999) defini-tion of "effective" is that "lives are transformed such that people are constantly enabled to become more Christ-like" (p. 15). By "highly effective," Barna means that these are:

> churches where the people are implementing Christianity more
> and more deeply, both on the corporate and individual levels.
> They are people who truly worship God on a regular basis. They
> are people who are consistently introducing non-Christians to
> Christ. They are learning and applying principles and truths of

the Christian faith to their lives. They are developing significant relationships with other believers, befriending, encouraging and holding each other accountable. They joyfully contribute their material possessions to ministries and individuals in need, for the glory of God. And they devote their time and energy to helping disadvantaged people. Cumulatively, these behaviors represent the Church in its fullest manifestation (p. 18).

Barna (1999) estimated that only 10–15% of the then approximately 300,000 Protestant churches in America (that is 30,000 to 45,000 churches) are highly effective by this definition.

More pertinent, however, to a discussion of the "Black Church" situation is the book *High Impact African American Churches* (Barna and Jackson, 2004). In generating the materials for this book they, via telephone, surveyed and interviewed African American adults, senior pastors of "Black churches," and Black teenagers over a number of years. From this database, several areas of effectiveness are articulated that led them to call these churches "high impact churches." I will discuss each of these below.

The first area of distinctness is **leadership**. According to Barna and Jackson (2004), effective "Black churches" (high impact) have a true leader at the helm. The characteristics of these leaders (strategies that enable pastors to direct a life-changing ministry) are:

- the pastor is an agent of change
- communication occurs that inspires
- leadership in a team concept
- refusal to micromanage the ministry
- investment in developing effective followers
- impact through collaboration
- the significance of longevity (greatest impact tends to

73

occur from years 5 through 14 of leadership in the congregation)
- always leading, always growing
- building the adaptable model

The second area of effectiveness concerns **discipleship**. According to Barna and Jackson (2004), these churches:

- have leadership for discipleship
- have a clear discipleship philosophy
- blend evangelism and discipleship
- provide practical theology
- offer many means of growing
- believe faith without works is dead
- has spiritual substance

The third area of high impact churches is **worship**. According to Barna and Jackson (2004), the four building blocks
of meaningful worship are:

- effective use of music
- strong leadership by a music director or team (there are
  three significant elements that the director or team does:
  (1) Focus worshipers' attention on God (2) Help people
  engage in intimate contact with a loving and holy God
  (3) Coordinate the musical selections and performances
  to facilitate a focus on and connection to God)
- effective use of biblical teaching or preaching
- consistent congregational engagement and response

A fourth area present in high impact churches is **effective
evangelism**. Barna and Jackson (2004) found five important

components that explained how the high impact churches facilitate effective evangelism. These are:

- begin with leadership; it is not a program, but a priority
- establish underlying philosophies
- develop an evangelistic culture
- equip the saints for multiplication
- reinforce people's efforts

The fifth area of high impact churches is a strategic focus on **families**. Six efforts are identified in this area. These are:

- intentional strategy
- attitude adjustment
- life transformation
- family ministry
- motivation of the congregation
- identity and unity

A sixth area of high impact churches is **holistic stewardship.** Under this rubric, Barna and Jackson (2004) list seven factors that are found in effective leaders who can motivate congregants to invest time, money, and energy toward spiritual outcomes. These factors are:

- a trustworthy environment
- a shared cause
- addressing urgent needs
- intimacy with the ministry
- effectiveness
- efficiency
- personal benefit

They feel that the more of the seven components listed above that a stewardship effort satisfies, the more successful it will be.

A seventh area characteristic of high impact churches is **serving the community**. These churches according to Barna and Jackson (2004) have the "ability to read the local culture and intuitively shift their ministry activity to addressing existing needs. This is demonstrated in the social and economic services provided by the church" (pp. 178–179).

The final area discussed that is characteristic of the high impact churches is the **facilitation of person-to-person connections**.

Barna and Jackson (2004) further stated that "the quality of leadership provided to a church is perhaps the single most significant factor in its ability to become a high impact ministry" (p. 194).

"Highly effective" and "high impact" churches are ones that respond well to and attend to the full range of needs of its members (including the psychological). These congregations would be similar to the liberation, missional, and fresh bread churches already mentioned.

Warren (1995) has introduced the idea of a "Purpose Driven Church." For him, the purpose driven church offers a new paradigm that he believes is biblically based and a healthy alternative to the traditional ways of churches. There are two essential components of this paradigm:

> First, it requires a new *perspective*. You must begin to look at everything your church does through the lens of five New Testament purposes and see how God intends for the church to balance all five purposes.
>
> Second, this paradigm requires a *process* for fulfilling the purposes of the church (p. 80; italics added).

The five purposes of a church that he lists are fellowship, discipleship, worship, ministry, and evangelism.

Elsewhere, Warren (1995, pp. 123–124) has stated that churches have historically taken on five basic shapes given the purposes they have emphasized the most. These five shapes (types) are:

- The Soul Winning Church. The pastor of such a congregation assumes the primary role of an evangelist and the congregation focuses mainly on saving souls.
- The Experiencing God Church. In this congregation, the pastor focuses primarily on worship and the congregation focuses primarily on "experiencing the presence and power of God in worship" (p. 123).
- The Family Reunion Church. The primary focus in this congregation is on fellowship.
- The Classroom Church. In this congregation, the pastor has teaching as the primary gift and thus emphasizes teaching and preaching and deemphasizes other tasks.
- The Social Conscience Church. In this congregation, the primary role of the pastor is that of a "prophet" and social reformer.

THE MEGACHURCH AS A TYPOLOGY

Protestant megachurches have been increasing rapidly in numbers and gaining research and media attention. Thumma (2005), for example, estimated that at the beginning of the 20th century there were a half dozen such churches and by 1960 there were sixteen. As of 2005, he reported that the number had reached 1210. *Christianity Today* (2005) gave the number as 1200, representing .03 percent of Protestant congregations. At its most basic descriptive level, a protestant megachurch is so designated when a congregation has 2,000 or more worship attendees in a week (Thumma, Travis and Bird 2005).

Thumma and his colleagues have been conducting research on the megachurch and have articles posted on the Hartford Institute for Religious Research website. In their most recent article, as of this publication, Thumma, Travis, and Bird (2005) have updated the original study by Thumma and are in the process of releasing a book entitled *Beyond Megachurch Myths: What can be Learned from America's Largest Churches*. In the article titled "Megachurches Today 2005: Summary of Research Findings," the following description is presented as characteristic of these congregations:

- Size is the primary definitive characteristic.
- The typical Protestant megachurch has an average attendance of 2,000 to 3000 members.
- At least 50% use multiple venues for worship as well as satellite locations to accommodate worshipers.
- The four states with the greatest concentration of megachurches are: California, Texas, Florida, and Georgia; these tend to be concentrated around the largest cities and most are located in the newer suburbs.
- Between 35 and 40% claim to be nondenominational.
- Nearly all hold multiple worship services.
- In describing the characteristics of their largest worship service, respondents gave the descriptions of "filled with a sense of God's presence," "inspirational," and "joyful." Most have included culturally relevant forms into these services. Most use contemporary forms of worship styles. Approximately 80% make use of electric guitar or bass and drums.
- Most of the churches (56%) describe their theological orientation as Evangelical.

- As to political outlook, over 50% described themselves as conservative and another 33% as somewhat conservative. Most were not considered "highly political."
- As to congregational identity, 70% strongly agreed that their church had a clear mission and purpose, while another 65% agreed that the church was spiritually vital and alive.
- They tend to have a significant multiracial presence. Fifty-six percent of those surveyed indicated that they were making intentional efforts to do so.
- They offer a wide variety of ministry programs and activities.
- As to member characteristics, they tend to be under 60 years old and often under 35, college graduates, generally married with children, and new to the congregation within the last five years.
- The senior pastor was considered a key component of the success of the congregation and 83% of the congregations in the survey indicated that the large growth occurred during the tenure of the current pastor.
- The average income in the last fiscal year of the survey period was approximately 6 million dollars. Hence, the average income for the 1,200 megachurches combined is approximately 7.2 billion dollars per year.
- The numerical success can be attributed to the fact that they attract and retain more persons over time than do other churches. Hence, the majority (58%) reported that evangelism and recruitment were key activities.
- The congregations founded after 1991 are more likely to be nondenominational and also less likely to describe themselves as traditional, moderate, Pentecostal, or charismatic.

- The more recently a megachurch was founded, the more likely that the pastor is younger and less formally educated.

The descriptions by Thumma et al of megachurches spanned racial lines, but he did not, in this article, focus extensively on Black or African American congregations.

In the popular arena, *Ebony Magazine* (2001) featured fifteen different African American megachurch congregations in an article titled "The New Megachurches." In their description, some of the primary, though not exclusive, characteristics of these megachurches are:

- the size of membership
- the number of services offered during Sunday
- their names
- the variety of ministries taking place

The megachurches featured in *Ebony* were the larger churches and thus had mostly memberships of 10,000 to 25,000 at the time of the publication. Of the fifteen congregations referenced in *Ebony*: two carried the name "Center," ten "Church," one "Temple," one "Cathedral," and one uses the name "Ministries." The date of founding ranges from 1834 to 1996. However, as also indicated by Thumma, the large membership is a relative recent phenomenon with six of these being founded since the 1970s.

As also noted by various writers, because of the size of membership and budget, these churches are able to offer a variety of ministries and activities that are geared to the needs and desires of the members.

In describing the megachurches, *Ebony* stated:

One sits on a tree-shaded suburban plot that could hold a small college. Another could comfortably accommodate the NBA final for it is in fact the former home of the Los Angeles Lakers. Still another owns "twin churches" and a helicopter that transports its pastors to different services on the same Sunday.

These and the other megachurches . . . are representative examples of a new trend in Black America that has caused conversions, talk and some controversy from Los Angeles to Atlanta and from New York to New Orleans.

Although the new megachurches differ in style and orientation, most are characterized by congregations of from 10,000 to 25,000 and spectacular buildings which house sanctuaries, day-care centers, bookstores, and health centers. Most resound with crowds and activities seven days a week, and most own businesses, subdivisions, and separate community activity buildings.

Some religious experts have questioned the emphasis on monumentality and have suggested that there is a danger of losing the gospel in the big sanctuaries and the wide variety of programs. But the male and female pastors of the new megachurches, almost all of whom have TV pastorates and feature high-tech video along with foot-tapping music, say they are creating a new church for a new century, and that a congregation can't do its full duty to its parishioners if it doesn't minister to all of their needs (pp. 148, 160).

Thumma (1996) estimated that while most of the megachurches are nondenominational, approximately 10% have ties with historically African American denominations.

In describing the overall phenomena of the megachurch, Thumma (1996) made the following analytical comments:

This new configuration of religious life is a result of the creative adaptation to a changing social situation. Megachurches as a social phenomenon can only be seen as a collective response to shifting social and cultural patterns of American society (p. 24).

Megachurches are not just a unique expression of baby boomer religion, "a new paradigm" religiously, nor are they the result of an overabundance of religious entrepreneurs. Rather changing cultural and social conditions have created a context in which this alternative form of religious organization has come to be seen as a viable option . . . It represents one of the most prominent religious patterns which have developed in relation to recent changes in American society. It is exactly this relevance which enabled most of the megachurches to reach their present size. They were able to adjust to a changing context in order to address the needs of their clientele (p. 25).

For the answer to why megachurches have become so popular and plentiful in the last several decades, one must examine their common characteristics in relation to the personal, social, and cultural reality of those who become megachurch members. These distinctive congregations must be seen in their cultural context in order to identify their appeal, beneath their obvious programmatic efforts (p. 25).

Mamiya (2006) in the report titled *Pulpit and Pew—Research on Pastoral Leadership* believes that African Americans have been disproportionately attracted to megachurches. While noting that adequate research has not been done in this area, he cited several possible reasons for this attraction: (a) the size of the congregation, (b) the charisma of the pastor, (c) the message, (d) the musical program, or (e) a combination of these factors. He also noted that Black megachurches are predominantly urban compared to White congregations which tend to be suburban. This observation is also made by Tucker-Worgs (2002), who has studied in detail the "Black megachurch" phenomenon.

The greater financial resources available to megachurches permit them to offer a variety of programs and activities to potentially meet the range of needs found in its membership and to do so in a more comprehensive manner. However, because a congregation is large and has access to greater resources does not necessarily ensure that its members are practicing or hearing the "true" gospel and practicing "healthy" Christianity.

As to determining who might be attracted to the megachurches psychologically and spiritually, it becomes difficult to do so because megachurches can theoretically fit all descriptions of types that have been presented. That is, they can be an entertainment/burn-up congregation, a containment/freeze-up congregation, or a liberation/fresh bread/missional/purpose driven congregation.

DENOMINATIONS AS A TYPOLOGY

As already mentioned in discussing the Lincoln and Mamiya descriptions, denominations can only be considered as a typology in a narrow sense. Denominations sprung up over time for a multiplicity of reasons. The interested reader may wish to consult the book by Mead (2001) (revised by Hill) entitled *Handbook of Denominations in the United States* which lists eighteen typologies. Using denominations as a typology, however, does not lend itself to any ready critique because the broad range of psychological and spiritual types is likely found within and across denominational lines.

BREAKOUT CHURCHES

This designation is given by Rainer (2005) and is based on research following much of the methodology used by Collins (2001) in the book *Good to Great* wherein several Fortune 500 companies were studied. This book contains a wealth of materials descriptive of churches that met the criteria for inclusion in the study. At its basic level, the screen for such churches in meeting the preliminary criteria and definitions were that they:

- had at least twenty-six conversions annually
- averaged a conversion ratio no higher than 20:1 at least one year since its breakout year
- had been declining or had reached a plateau for several years before the breakout year or was experiencing stagnation
- had broken out of its slump and sustained its growth for several years
- sustained the slump and reversal; breakout took place under the same pastor
- had made a clear and positive impact on the community since the breakout point.

The leaders of the breakout churches had several characteristics that differentiated them from the comparison group and these were (pp. 66–67):

- displayed fierce biblical faithfulness through doctrinal truths while practicing these through their preaching, teaching, leadership, and ministry
- had an average tenure at the congregations of 21.6 years
- exhibited confident humility without the appearance of arrogance or haughtiness
- accepted responsibility for their ministry and did not blame others when things did not go well
- showed "unconditional love" to the members served
- were persistent and did not view a setback as a failure

- always included an evangelistic passion
- showed concern beyond their own tenure and lifetime

MALPHURS' DESCRIPTIONS

Aubrey Malphurs (2007) in the book *A New Kind of Church* explores the changing nature of the church and gives some general descriptions of this institution. Malphurs' descriptions are not based on empirical research. Four descriptions will be mentioned here, but only two of these will be discussed. The two that will only be mentioned are called the "Thinking Church" and the "Strategizing Church." These two represent, more or less, the strategies used by congregations in developing and evaluating their ministries rather than a church type as such.

The two types that will be briefly discussed are as follow:

- The Connecting Church. This church type is so described because it attempts to operate in a manner that allows it to effectively relate to the culture and to be relevant to it.
- The Serving Church. Based on both Old and New Testament scriptural references, Malphurs labels this church type as such because it seeks to implement the concept of servanthood in its ministry to lost people.

BEYOND TYPES

As already noted, the church types (excluding the ones described in the book of Revelation) generally come from descriptions which are found in sources that are not based on research or detailed academic treatises. While the use of types as descriptors provides helpful information and gives cause to reflect, the categorizations can be and have been criticized. These singular descriptions may assist us in understanding a specific congregation or a singular phenomenon, but fall short of an adequate explanation of the broader church or "Black Church" community.

Specifically, Lincoln and Mamiya (1990) state that:

> The problem of a single, nondialectical typological view of black churches is that they tend to categorize and stereotype black churches into rigid pigeonhole categories like "other-worldly"; they miss the historical dynamism of institutions moving back and forth in response to certain issues or social conditions (p. 15).

Dulles (2002), writing from a Roman Catholic point of view, would agree with Lincoln and Mamiya and stated that:

> In selecting the term "models" . . . , I wish to indicate my conviction that the Church, like other theological realities, is a mystery. Mysteries are realities of which we cannot speak directly.
>
> The peculiarity of models, as contrasted with aspects, is that we cannot integrate them into a single synthetic vision on the level of articulate, categorical thought. In order to do justice to the various aspects of the Church, as a complex reality, we must work simultaneously with different models (p. 2).

Given Lincoln and Mamiya's and Dulles' cautions and concerns regarding types, consideration will now be given to a discussion of models of the church. (These models are portrayed in Table 3.)

Table 3
CHURCH MODELS

Nelsen and Nelsen	Lincoln and Mamiya	Dulles
Assimilation or Isolation-Integration	Priestly vs. Prophetic	Institution
Compensatory	Other-Worldly vs. This-Worldly	Mystical Communion
Ethnic Community-Prophetic	Universalism vs. Particularism	Sacrament
		Herald
	Communal vs. Privatistic	Servant
	Charismatic vs. Bureaucratic	
	Resistance vs. Accomodation	

CHURCHES AS MODELS

Three models are summarized by Nelsen and Nelsen (1975) who believe they can be derived from a summary of theoretical treatments and/or research on "Black churches." These models are the Assimilation or Isolation-Integration Model, the Compensatory Model, and the Ethnic Community-Prophetic Model.

The Assimilation Model is used when describing or viewing the "Black Church" either as a stumbling block to Blacks assimilating in the larger society or when it is isolated from the larger society. In this model, the church is seen as uninvolved in civic and political matters and religion is mainly seen as "other-worldly." Writers such as E. Franklin Frazier, Kenneth Clark, and Gary T. Mark are viewed by Nelsen and Nelsen (1975) as typical of representing this approach.

The Compensatory Model characterizes the "Black Church" as allowing participants within its structure to gain and have the power, respect, etc., that cannot be found or gained in larger society. Writers such as St. Clair Drake, Horace Cayton, and Gunnar Myrdal are representative of this model according to Nelsen and Nelsen.

The third model, the Ethnic Community-Prophetic, characterizes the church as focusing on matters of race and ways to improve the conditions of Blacks within the larger society. Writers such as Benjamin Mays, Joseph Nicholson, Gayraud Wilmore, and James Cone are reflective of this model, according to Nelsen and Nelsen.

The Assimilation church is likely to be the setting where individuals who are low on ethnic identity are most comfortable. Such individuals are likely to feel some discomfort with their African heritage and traditions. Those representative of the Compensatory Model are likely individuals who are striving for self-actualization, which they feel they cannot or have not achieved in the broader society. Individuals within the context of the Ethnic Community-Prophetic Model are likely to be those who are heavily ethnically identified, feel a high sense of self-actualization, and are comfortable with fighting for full legal rights for all.

Building on the work of Nelsen and Nelsen (1975), Lincoln and Mamiya (1990) proposed a dialectical model of the "Black Church" in which they saw churches as in a constant series of dialectical tensions. To them the dialectics hold polar opposites in tension, constantly shifting between the poles in time. Lincoln and Mamiya's six pairs of dialectics with related polar opposites are:

- the dialectic between the priestly and the prophetic functions
- the dialectic between other-worldly versus this-worldly
- the dialectic between universalism and particularism
- the dialectic between the communal and the privatistic
- the dialectic between charismatic versus bureaucratic
- the dialectic between resistance versus accommodation

Each of these will be discussed below.

The Dialectic between the Priestly and the Prophetic Functions. Priestly functions refer to activities involving worship and the spiritual lives of members. Hence, church maintenance activities are the major area for this pole. Prophetic functions refer to involvement in political and wider community activities. For Lincoln and Mamiya, churches are involved in both, but vary as to which end of the pole is the major emphasis at a given point in time.

The Dialectic between Other-worldly versus This-worldly. This dialectic reflects the orientation of the church toward the world. Those with an "other-worldly" orientation are primarily concerned with heaven, life after death, eternal life, and what some have labeled "pie-in-the-sky." The "this-worldly" orientation reflects involvement in activities of this world such as politics and things that have been labeled the "here and now."

The Dialectic between Universalism and Particularism. The tension found in this dialectic focuses on the church's universalism of the Christian message versus the specifics of racism demonstrated by "White" Christianity and issues stemming from the larger society.

The Dialectic between the Communal and the Privatistic. This dialectic involves whether the "Black Church" is oriented with all aspects of the lives of its members or whether there is a withdrawal from the larger community resulting in a primary focus on only the religious needs of its membership.

The Dialectic between Charismatic versus Bureaucratic. The charismatic pole of this dialectic refers to the focus of the church on "gifts" and the oral tradition (speaking abilities). The bureaucratic pole involves developing central headquarters, record keeping, etc.

The Dialectic between Resistance versus Accommodation. The pole of resistance refers to the "Black Church" affirming the African/Black heritage—both self-determination and self-affir-mation. For Lincoln and Mamiya (1990), accommodation means "to be influenced by the larger society and to take part in aspects of it, however marginal that participation may be" (p. 15).

PSYCHOLOGY AND THE DIALECTIC MODEL

The dialectic model is not one that readily lends itself to a psychological analysis given that it reflects a continuum.

DULLES' MODELS

Dulles (2002), writing from a Roman Catholic perspective, presented five models of the church which are discussed below.

The Church as Institution. In this model, the church is de-scribed as "a system in which the institutional element is treated as primary" (p. 27). Under this model, the church teaches, sanc-tifies, and rules with the authority of Christ.

The Church as Mystical Communion. In describing this model, Dulles sees the church as God's people or Christ's Body, growing into the final perfection of the Kingdom.

The Church as Sacrament. In this model, the church is viewed and described as "the visible manifestation of the grace of Christ in human community" (p. 81).

The Church as Herald. In this model, Dulles sees the church as one that "takes on an authoritarian role, proclaiming the gospel as a divine message to which the world must humbly listen" (p. 81).

The Church as Servant. In the final model put forth by Dulles, "the servant church is the community who confirms mankind in its freedom to fashion its future, protesting the pretensions to ultimacy in any human structures and suffering with men in the struggle against the power of evil" (pp. 87–88).

CONCLUSION

As has been shown in this chapter, categorizations of the institutional church abound. In reviewing and considering church types and models, it becomes clear that the church in general and what is known as the "Black Church" in particular, given its history and evolution over time in America, is a complex "organism"— a complexity that continues. We would do well to keep that in mind as we continue to seek to understand and improve this unique institution. Speaking to this issue, Lincoln and Mamiya (1990) state:

Unless one understands that black churches are involved in a dynamic series of dialectical tensions, a serious misunderstanding of these institutions can occur because the usual tendency is to collapse the dialectic and assert one side of the polarity, which often results in a simplistic view . . .

The dialectical model allows for a more objective analysis of black churches as social institutions because it takes a broader, more comprehensive perspective. It moves beyond the simplistic positive or negative assessments of personal observation and places black churches along a dynamic continuum allowing for change in response to changing social conditions (p. 16).

REFERENCES

Barna, G. (1999). *The Habits of Highly Effective Churches*. Ventura: Regal.

Barna, G. and H. R. Jackson Jr. (2004). *High Impact African American Churches*. Ventura: Regal.

Carson, C. and P. Holloran (Editors) (1998). *A Knock at Midnight: Inspirations from the Great Sermons of Reverend Martin Luther King, Jr.* New York: Warner Books.

_____ (Editors) (1998). *A Knock at Midnight. Original Recordings of Reverend Dr. Martin Luther King, Jr.* New York: Intellectual Properties Management.

Collins, J. (2001). *Good to Great*. New York: HarperBusiness.

Dulles, A. C. (2002). *Models of the Church*. New York: Image Books-Doubleday.

Feucht, O. E. (1981). *Everyone a Minister*. St. Louis: Concordia.

Gibbs, E. (2000). *Church Next: Quantum Changes in How We Do Ministry*. Downers Grove: InterVarsity Press.

"Go Figure." (August 2005). *Christianity Today*. 49, p. 22.

King, M. L. Jr. (1998). *A Knock at Midnight*. In Carson, C. and P. Holloran (Editors) (2000). *A Knock at Midnight: Inspirations from the Great Sermons of Reverend Martin Luther King, Jr.* New York: Warner Books.

Kunjufu, J. (1994). *Adam! Where are You? Why Most Black Men Don't Go to Church*. Chicago: African American Images.

Lincoln, C. E. and L. H. Mamiya (1990). *The Black Church in the African American Experience*. Durham: Duke University Press.

Malphurs, A. (2007). *A New Kind of Church: Understanding Models of Ministry for the 21st Century.* Grand Rapids: Baker Books.

Mamiya, L. (2006). *Pulpit & Pew—Research on Pastoral Leadership. River of Struggle, River of Freedom—Trends Among Black Churches and Black Pastoral Leadership* (Pulpit Research Reports). Durham: Duke Divinity School (www. pulpitandpew.duke.edu).

Mead F. S. (Revised by S. S. Hill) (2001). *Handbook of Denominations in the United States New Eleventh Edition.* Nashville: Abingdon.

Nelsen, H. M. and A. K. Nelsen (1975). *Black Church in the Sixties.* Lexington: The University Press of Kentucky.

Rainer, T. S. (2005). *Breakout Churches.* Grand Rapids: Zondervan.

"The New Megachurches." (December 2001). *Ebony.* 57, 148–60.

Thumma, S. (1996). *Exploring the Megachurch Phenomena: their characteristics and cultural context.* Hartford Institute for Religion Research. http://hirr.hartsem.edu/bookshelf/thumma_article2.html

Thumma, S., D. Travis, and W. Bird (2005). *Megachurches Today 2005: Summary of Research Findings.* Hartford Institute of Religion Research. http://hirr.hartsem.edu/megachurch/megastoday2005-summaryreport.html

Tucker-Worgs, T. (2002). *Get on Board, Little Children, There's Room for Many More: The Black Megachurch Phenomenon.* In *Journal Inward, Journey Outward. A Special Journal of Interdenominational Theological Center.* 29, 177–202.

Warren, R. (1995). *The Purpose Driven Church*. Grand Rapids: Zondervan.

CHAPTER 4

Types of Members

*"And I, brethren, could not speak unto you
as unto spiritual, but as unto carnal,
even as unto babes in Christ."*

1 CORINTHIANS 3:1

*"I beseech you therefore, brethren,
by the mercies of God, that ye present your bodies
a living sacrifice, holy, acceptable unto God,
which is your reasonable service."*

ROMANS 12:1

*"Now there are diversities of gifts,
but the same Spirit. And there are differences
of administrations, but the same Lord.
And there are diversities of operations,
but it is the same God which worketh all in all."*

1 CORINTHIANS 12:4–6

INTRODUCTION

Just as there are types and models of churches (which were discussed in the preceding chapter), there are also types of individuals and titles represented in the church. Names and titles are worthy of review and discussion for at least two reasons. First, names and titles can have both positive and negative impacts on behaviors, perceptions, and expectations within the church community. A person will behave in their personal and corporate lives according to what he or she thinks he or she is supposed to be.

Secondly, names and titles need to be examined as to which are of biblical origin and the impacts of their use/misuse. This is critical because one reacts to the labels and behaves in conformity to what one believes the labels mean and connote. I believe that the extrabiblical and nonbiblical meanings given to several of the terms commonly used already have and continue to impede the overall impact and influence of the church community. In examining these terms, the meaning of most of the terms in the Greek language will also be given since the New Testament was basically originally written in Greek.

THE ARRAY OF NAMES

Within the church community, one can find an array of names or titles represented, such as:

- Pastor
- Preacher
- Minister
- Clergy
- Laity
- Deacon
- Apostle

- Teacher
- Evangelist
- Prophet
- Prophetess
- Bishop
- Elder
- Psalmist

- Healer
- Reverend
- Sister
- Brother
- Mother
- Father
- Saint

Preacher and Pastor

In everyday situations, these terms are frequently used interchangeably; however, biblically speaking they are not designated as such. In the New Testament, the Greek word for pastor is *poimen*, which means shepherd (Strong, 1996). One of the primary words for preacher in the New Testament is *kerusso* and means to herald as a public crier; to proclaim; or to publish (Strong, 1996).

Within the Black community and the "Black Church" the person who is a pastor is often more revered for preaching than for pastoring. As noted by Hamilton (1972), preaching is one of the qualities that is most desirable and reinforced. I believe that this overemphasis on preaching has often led many pastors to neglect the "shepherding" and leadership aspects of their roles.

An additional widespread belief about preaching is that it is an activity to be geared toward believers and within a church setting. Speaking in contrast to this belief, Douglas (1971) in *The New Bible Dictionary* indicated that preaching in the early church was an activity geared toward nonbelievers. He stated,

In the New Testament, preaching is 'the public proclamation of Christianity to the non-Christian world' (C. H. Dodd, *The Apostolic Preaching and its Developments*, 1944, p, 7). It is not religious discourse to a closed group of initiates, but open proclamation of God's redemptive activity in and through Jesus Christ. The current understanding of preaching as biblical exposition and exhortation, while a valid extension of the term, has tended to obscure its primitive meaning (p. 1023).

In the New Testament, there are five Greek words that designate "preach" according to *The New Strong's Exhaustive Concordance of the Bible* (Strong, 1996). These words are *kerusso* (to herald as a public crier, especially divine truth; to proclaim or publish); *euaggelizo* (to announce good news; to evangelize especially the gospel; to declare or bring good tidings); *diaggello* (to herald thoroughly; to declare; to signify); *kataggello* (to proclaim, promulgate, declare, shew, speak of, or teach, and *laleo* (to talk; that is, utter words; say; speak after).

While each of these words does not apply to all believers, a form of "preaching" has been and can be done by the general body of believers. For example, in Acts 8:4, "Therefore they that were scattered abroad went every where preaching the word," is such an occurrence. The Greek word used here for preaching is *euaggelizo* which means to announce good tidings.

Furthermore, the emphasis on preaching to those who are already believers devalues what is the main need and biblical mandate for a believer, and that is to be taught and developed as a disciple. It also ignores the fact that, biblically speaking, preaching is not one of the stated qualifications for the person desiring the office of a bishop (pastor). That is, preaching is not listed in 1 Timothy 3:1–7, but on the contrary, teaching is mentioned in 1 Timothy 3:2. These beliefs about preaching have also undoubtedly contributed to the development and maintenance of the "great" preaching tradition within the "Black Church." Often a typical greeting that pastors give each other is not "hey, Pastor," but "hey, Preacher."

This widespread belief, that preaching can only be done by certain Christians and should primarily occur within church settings, has probably led to the development of a group of "specialists" who take extreme pride in exhibiting their "art form." *Ebony* magazine's historical annual listings of the fifteen greatest preachers also contributed to this phenomenon of elevating preaching over pastoring, particularly in "Black churches."

Minister

The term "minister" is often likewise used interchangeably with pastor and preacher. Yet, biblically speaking, the word "minister" does not carry the same meaning as pastor or preacher. More problematic, however, is that the title "minister" is often used exclusively for pastors and "preachers."

According to Strong (1996), the word "minister" comes from the Greek word *diakonos* which means an attendant; or a waiter at tables. Feucht (1981), in a chapter titled "Wanted: A Functional Ministry" of the book *Everyone a Minister*, stated:

> The church is all of God's people in ministry sharing the
> Gospel with people of all nations. The church is more than a
> place for a certain ritual for worship. It is especially not an in-
> stitution. The church is reborn flesh-and-blood people who are
> God's agents of reconciliation (2 Corinthians 5:17–21). The
> church is a living organism.
>
> All of God's people belong to the New Testament "minis-
> terium." The word "minister" is usually equated with "clergy."
> It is not so in the Bible. In Scripture it is closely linked to the
> Greek word *diakonia*. This may be translated "service" or

"ministry." And it is by no means restricted to what a pastor does in a church building (p. 83).

The misuse and narrow use of the term "minister" in church settings can have detrimental effects on the overall effectiveness of the church. Warren (1995) also expresses a similar view of the often limited view of ministry.

Thus, to be biblically accurate and to generate maximum church effectiveness, there must be a change in the belief that only certain people are ministers. Indeed, all Christians are ministers in the biblical sense of the word.

Clergy and Laity

These terms are extra-biblical and evolved over time in church history; they are used to draw a separation between the pulpit and the pew. As the institutional church became more hierarchal, the terms "clergy" and "laity" came into vogue. However, as already noted, in early church history (The New Testament period), everyone who was a Christian was considered a minister and at some points all believers preached the Gospel (see Acts 8:4). Speaking to this issue of clergy and laity, Feucht (1981) stated:

> It is most often used in regard to personnel in the church. The opposite of layman is clergyman. This usually means the minister of a parish. The current use goes back in history to the appointment of priests by bishops and originated in the post-apostolic life of the church. The term "pastor" means shepherd and the flock he cares for are the laity (p. 54).

Deacon

The word "deacon" (Greek word *diakoneo*) according to Strong (1996) means to be an attendant; to wait upon menially

101

or as a host, friend, or teacher; to minister unto, or serve. It is a biblical word and deacons who are properly selected and carry out the full biblical responsibility of this role are powerful within the body of Christ. I have treated this topic in detail in another source (see June, 1999).

Apostle, Teacher, Evangelist, and Prophet

Apostle, teacher, evangelist, and prophet, along with pastor (already discussed) are the fivefold gifted individuals spoken of in Ephesians 4:11, as well as in other parts of the New Testament. Note, however, that in the Ephesians passage, it is explicitly stated as to why these five gifted individuals were given to the church and that is: "For the perfecting of the saints, for the work of the ministry, for the edifying of the body of Christ: Till we all come in the unity of the faith, and of the knowledge of the Son of God, unto a perfect man, unto the measure of the stature of the fulness of Christ: That we henceforth be no more children, tossed to and fro, and carried about with every wind of doctrine, by the sleight of men, and cunning craftiness, whereby they lie in wait to deceive" (Ephesians 4:12–14).

While there are similarities in these terms, each has different biblical meanings. An "apostle" (Greek word *apostolos*) means an ambassador of the gospel; a messenger, or one that is sent (Strong, 1996). A "teacher" (Greek word *didaskalos*) means an instructor (Strong, 1996). "Evangelist" (Greek word *euaggelistes*) means a preacher of the gospel (Strong, 1996). A "prophet" (Greek word *prophetes*) means a foreteller; an inspired speaker (Strong, 1996). The word "prophet" is found in both the Old and New Testaments but the meaning changed over the two periods of time.

Prophetess

This word is found in both the Old and New Testaments. In the New Testament, the Greek word is *prophetis*, which according to Strong (1996) means a female foreteller or an inspired woman. Today, this word is increasingly being used and is taking on new and often unclear meanings.

Bishop and Elder

The Greek word for bishop is *episkopos* which means a superintendent; a Christian officer in general charge of the church; an overseer (Strong, 1996). The word "elder" (Greek word *presbuteros*) means older. Probably, one of the more acceptable distinctions regarding these words is given by Scofield (1998). He states:

> Elder (Gk. *presbuteros*) and bishop (Gk. *episkopos=overseer*) designate the same office (cp. v. 7; Acts 20:17; cp. v. 28), the former referring to the man, the latter to a function of the office. The eldership in the apostolic churches was usually plural; there is no instance of only one elder in a local church. The functions of the elders are: to rule (1 Tim. 3:4-5; 5:17); to teach (1 Tim. 5:17); to guard the body of revealed truth from perversion and error (Ti. 1:9); and to oversee the church as a shepherd of his flock (Jn. 21:16; Acts 20:28; Heb. 13:17; 1 Pet 5:2). Elders are made or set in the churches by the Holy Spirit (Acts 20:28), but great stress is laid in the N.T. upon their appointment (Acts 14:23; Ti. 1:5). In Titus and 1 Timothy the qualifications of an elder become part of the Scriptures for the guidance of the churches themselves in such appointments (1 Tim. 3:1-7) (p. 1524).

Psalmist

This is an Old Testament term and was used in reference to David (see 2 Samuel 23:1). The Hebrew word for psalmist is *zamiyr* (Strong, 1996). Today, this title is resurfacing within church settings.

Healer

Healings is one of the gifts of the Holy Spirit, but the designation of a healer is not a New Testament designation. Hence, the emphasis in Scripture seems to be on the activity of healing, not the person who assists in the healing process. Unfortunately, too often the emphasis, or overemphasis is on the person and less on the activity as a spiritual gift.

Reverend

There is only one use of the word "reverend" in Scripture in most English translations of the Bible and that is found in Psalm 111:9 which states: "He sent redemption unto his people: he hath commanded his covenant for ever: holy and reverend is his name." Contextually, the term in Scripture is used in reference to God, not humans.

Many will argue that the use of Reverend is merely a term of respect. They will further argue that it is an appropriate designation for one who has been "called" of God and to denote someone who is separated to preach the Gospel and/or is a pastor. While these arguments are persuasive, however, this term as is currently used is extra-biblical and came about as the church became more hierarchal.

Sister and Brother

Sister and brother are affectionate terms and are used both biblically and in contemporary congregations to describe female and male believers of Christ, respectively.

Mother and Father

Mother, in the Bible, generally refers to a female parent. Within many "Black churches," "mother" takes on an additional meaning and refers to older women who have been faithful to the congregation and who have typically served for a number of years with distinction. Thus, "mother" has become a title of endearment, distinction, and special honor.

Within the church, the term "Father" does not have a similar meaning beyond a parent as does the designation "mother." However, in the New Testament, both Jesus and the New Testament writers refer to God as Father. Jesus also states in reference to God, that "God is a Spirit: and they that worship him must worship him in spirit and in truth" (John 4:24). In the model prayer, Jesus told His followers: "After this manner therefore pray ye: Our Father which art in heaven, Hallowed be thy name" (Matthew 6:9).

While the use of "Father" in reference to God is biblically sanctioned, the use of the term currently with "Black churches" has raised some concerns. That is, some have wondered whether this may be one of the reasons why some Black males have trouble identifying with God as a loving Father, given the estrangement of many Black males from their biological fathers. This is a concern worth attending to, but the solution to this concern is not to stop using the term in reference to God; rather this must become a sensitivity factor and has implications for how we teach and reach out to youths, both male and female.

Saint

In the New Testament, "saint" (Greek word *hagios*) means sacred, consecrated, or holy. The word is applied to all believers, not a select few, as is often the case. Many church settings are uncomfortable with this term.

CONCLUSION

As mentioned at the outset, the main reason for discussing these words is to challenge the church community to seriously consider and reflect on how we may have strayed from the original meanings of many of these terms. Additionally, we need to carefully examine how the misuse of these terms/titles can and quite often impede the Body of Christ in being fully effective. When one believes that only certain believers are ministers, that only certain Christians are saints, that only certain people can "preach," that preaching is primarily for a closed audience, and so on, such beliefs will result in seriously limiting the churches' reach and impact. Moreover, these misconceptions will also influence the behaviors of its members in a negative fashion with both spiritual and psychological implications.

As consideration is given to the use of these terms and titles, it should be remembered that Jesus on one occasion harshly criticized the hypocrisy and overuse of titles and/or positions:

Then spake Jesus to the multitude, and to his disciples, Saying, The scribes and the Pharisees sit in Moses' seat: All therefore whatsoever they bid you observe, that observe and do; but do not ye after their works: for they say, and do not. For they bind heavy burdens and grievous to be borne, and lay them on men's shoulders; but they themselves will not move them with one of their fingers. But all their works they do for to be seen of men: they make broad their phylacteries, and enlarge the borders of their garments, And love the uppermost rooms at feasts, and the chief seats in the synagogues, And greetings in the markets, and to be called of men, Rabbi, Rabbi. But be not ye called Rabbi: for one is your Master, even Christ; and all ye are brethren. And call no man your father upon the earth: for one is your Father, which is in heaven. Neither be ye called masters: for one is your Master, even Christ. But he that is greatest among you shall be your servant. And whosoever shall exalt himself shall be abased; and he that shall humble himself shall be exalted (Matthew 23:1–12).

While I fully understand how over time the institutional church has come to have the structures and titles it has, it is time to reconsider where we are in light of Scripture. We must critically examine whether we have created the church in our image as opposed to what Jesus Christ intended. The emphasis in Scripture is not on titles, names, or positions, but rather upon service. Let us continually strive to live up to this expectation.

References

Douglas, J. (1971). *The New Bible Dictionary.* Grand Rapids: W. B. Eerdmans.

Feucht, O. E. (1981). *Everyone a Minister.* St. Louis: Concordia.

Hamilton, C. V. (1972). *The Black Preacher in America.* New York: William Morrow.

June, L. N. (1999). *The Deacon's Role.* In June, L.N. and M. Parker, *Evangelism and Discipleship in African American Churches.* Grand Rapids: Zondervan.

Scofield, C. I. (Editor) (1998). *The New Scofield Study Bible: Authorized King James Version.* New York: Oxford.

Strong, J. (1996). *The New Strong's Exhaustive Concordance of the Bible.* Nashville: Thomas Nelson.

Warren, R. (1995). *The Purpose Driven Church.* Grand Rapids: Zondervan.

PART 3
CHURCH SETTINGS

The Historical and Contemporary
Contributions of the Pastor and
Church Setting in Meeting the
Psychological Needs
of Individuals

■

Rituals, Offerings, Songs,
and Prayers

■

Innocent but Potentially
Detrimental Statements,
Concepts, and Beliefs

CHAPTER 5

The Historical and Contemporary Contributions of the Pastor and Church Setting in Meeting the Psychological Needs of Individuals

*"And I will give you pastors according
to mine heart, which shall feed you
with knowledge and understanding."*
JEREMIAH 3:15

*"Let us hold fast the profession of our faith without
wavering; (for he is faithful that promised;) And let us
consider one another to provoke unto love and to
good works: Not forsaking the assembling of
ourselves together, as the manner of some is;
but exhorting one another: and so much the more,
as ye see the day approaching."*
HEBREWS 10:23–25

*"I Jesus have sent mine angel to testify unto you these
things in the churches. I am the root and the offspring
of David, and the bright and morning star."*
REVELATION 22:16

INTRODUCTION

In chapter one, the unique and important role historically and contemporarily of the "Black Church" within American society was discussed. In this chapter, the focus will be on the Black pastor/preacher and the "Black Church" and how these two entities have aided in meeting both the overall spiritual and psychological needs of the members.

THE CONTRIBUTIONS OF THE PASTOR IN MEETING PSYCHOLOGICAL NEEDS

The Black pastor has historically been and in many cases continues to be preacher, poet, exhorter, teacher, "social worker," "psychologist," businessperson, politician, orator, civil rights leader, and community organizer. Hamilton (1972) stated:

Black preachers have always been pacifiers, passive resisters, and vigilantes. And each type has had, and continues to have to this day, substantial following in the black communities. They have this in common: They have all been leaders of their people—people needing comfort, instruction, encouragement and guidance. At some point during slavery, the various preachers filled, in their own ways, these needs (p. 68).

Woodson (1921) in the book *The History of the Negro Church* likewise noted the multiple roles that the Black pastor/preacher has occupied over the years as well as their genius. Part of the reason for the multiple roles has historically been that the pastor was invariably one of the most influential and articulate members of Black church society; frequently they were the most educated members of the Black community. Thus, the community and congregation demanded and, at minimum, expected them to be available to assist with their various needs.

The Black pastor was and still often remains a "counselor" to those facing family, marital, and personal difficulties. Moreover, the pastor has traditionally played a role in helping persons and families deal with death and grief issues. Their sermons often speak to these difficulties, as well as to issues of oppression and racism and thus provide hope in the midst of trials and tribulations through their teaching and sermons.

Preaching Styles. As has already been noted, the Black pastor in America developed and utilized a unique style of preaching and presenting messages. Mitchell (1979) in the book *Black Preaching* articulated this style. The style that developed is one which encourages the audience to be participatory. It relates to the deep emotions of the individual and often results in many worshipers crying, shouting, and showing various types of emotional expressions. It is what some have labeled "the call and response" style.

Mitchell (1979) saw in Black preaching the carrying on of a cultural tradition and a set of unique styles that have developed over time. He stated:

The preaching tradition of the Black Fathers did not spring into existence suddenly. It was developed after a long and often

quite disconnected series of contacts between the Christian
gospel variously interpreted and men caught up in the Black
experience of slavery and oppression. To this experience and
this gospel they brought their own culture and folkways. In
ways more unique and powerful than they or we dreamed until
recently, they developed a Black religious tradition. Very
prominent in that Black religious tradition were Black culture
sermons and the way Black men delivered and responded to
them (p. 65).

In his analysis of Black preaching, Mitchell (1979) listed two
principles of effective Black preaching: "The first is that one
must declare the gospel in the language and culture of the people
—the vernacular . . . The second hermeneutic principle is that
the gospel must speak to the contemporary man and his needs"
(p. 29).

Hamilton (1972) further noted that two of the greatest com-
pliments one could pay to Black preachers were: (1) that they
know their Bible well and (2) that they can really preach.

Much earlier than Mitchell, Pipes (1951) also analyzed
Black preaching styles in the book *Say Amen, Brother!* His focus was on what he called "old-time Negro preaching." In this
work, several sermons are transcribed and analyses of them are
presented. In many ways, his analysis is less positive than that
of Mitchell and Hamilton.

Black preaching is still an art form that has many unique
and positive features. However, it is unfortunate that in some circles and at certain times, the style of preaching has become as important (and sometimes more so) as the content of the message.
For some, "preaching" has not occurred unless it is done in a certain manner. There is much psychology in some preaching styles
and those who employ them know it and can cater to it.

The Psychology in Preaching. What is the psychology in Black preaching? I would suggest that there are at least two ways to describe Black preaching. First, there is the negative aspect. This negative and potentially detrimental aspect plays on and deliberatively seeks the emotions of the people. Those who employ this method of preaching may or may not be genuine. Such individuals know well the language, idioms, and culture of the people and congregation; they know well how to create an atmosphere that is capable of drawing people into an experience. In the presence of such "preaching," if one would withdraw from the experience and become an observer, one would probably describe what is happening as devoid of much substance and content.

From such a vantage point, the major goal of the "preaching" would seemingly be to create an experience, a happening. One would find it difficult to differentiate some of what occurs in such a service from what one would see at a major concert or other entertainment events. This type of "preaching" fits King's description of what often occurs in what he calls the "Burn-up Church." Persons who do this non-genuinely are using the people for their own benefits—whether to "fleece the flock" or for some other motive.

The preacher or pastor who does this genuinely is likely to be one who believes out of custom or tradition that this style must be used and this atmosphere must be created in order to have a "real" worship service or experience. This person is not trying to "fleece the flock" but is doing what is expected or feels appropriate. It is also important to note that the congregation also plays a critical role in maintaining this "preaching" style, tradition, and expectation. The effect on the congregation, emotionally or psychologically, often is the same whether done genuinely or non-genuinely. The congregation leaves "feeling good," having had an emotional experience,

having undergone catharsis, and possibly having engaged in a
worship experience.

The positive angle to this phenomenon is the situation
wherein deep emotions are felt, one leaves feeling good, but it
was not deliberately sought. Here, it was the by-product, not
the end goal of "worshiping."

I have observed both situations. The former at its extreme is
one in which the high clamor or music, the loud voices, and often the musical instruments dominate the scene. Persons are encouraged to participate actively whether one wants to or not. If
one does not engage actively into what is happening, one may
be made to feel that they are not "religious" or "saved." Statements often come from the pastor/preacher such as: "Anything
dead needs to be buried," "Can I get an Amen," and so on. Thus
in this environment, the outward expressions of emotion become
equated with worshiping and being a Christian and vice versa.

THE CONTRIBUTIONS OF THE CHURCH
IN MEETING PSYCHOLOGICAL NEEDS

The church—whatever the primary racial or ethnic make-
up—is a unique institution (organism). Individuals who make
up the church come from all walks of life with all kinds of
needs, desires, goals, agonies, and hurts. Given these various
needs and emotions and placed in the hands of those with
wrong motives, unsuspecting persons can be abused or misused.
History has given us some chilling examples.

While on the one hand, people with needs, desires, goals,
agonies, and hurts can be abused or misused, these same set
of conditions or circumstances gives the church setting its greatest potential to be a "healing community." No other institution
(organism) can fulfill the multiplicity of human needs in one
setting that a true church can.

The "Black Church" has historically been a spiritual and unique psychological sustaining force for Black people. Many have observed that, without God and the "Black Church," Blacks in America would not have survived the horrors of the middle passage and slavery. From all indications, and contrary to some observers, the historical faith of Black people as practiced in Christianity was authentic and genuine. It was "other-worldly," but also "this-worldly." It allowed individuals to sustain hope, bear pain, endure agony, and maintain a sense of sanity—with the hope and belief that a better day was coming by and by. Even those who do not share this faith would have to admit as history unfolded that a better day did come for Black people.

The historical "Black Church" had such a profound impact on the lives of the Black community that various psychological needs were met within its setting. The "Black Church" in its early American state was similar to traditional African Christianity in that it was a way of life and thus permeated a person's whole being. There was no room for the compartmentalizing or division that became more typical of 20th- and early 21st-century America.

In the book *African Religions and Philosophy*, Mbiti (1970) made the following comments speaking both to our African traditions and the more modern-day situation:

Africans are notoriously religious, and each people has its own religious system with a set of beliefs and practices. Religion permeates into all the departments of life so fully that it is not easy or possible always to isolate it (p. 1).

African peoples do not know how to exist without religion. One of the sources of severe strain for Africans exposed to modern change is the increasing process (through education,

urbanization and industrialization) by which individuals become detached from their traditional environment . . . It is not
enough to learn and embrace a faith which is active once a
week, either on Sunday or Friday, while the rest of the week is
virtually empty. It is not enough to embrace a faith which is
confined to a church building or mosque, which is locked up
six days and opened only once or twice a week. Unless Christianity and Islam fully occupy the whole person as much as, if
not more than, traditional religions do, most converts to these
faiths will continue to revert to their old beliefs and practices
for perhaps six days a week. . . .

Since traditional religions occupy the whole person and the
whole of his life, conversion to new religions like Christianity
and Islam must embrace his language, thought patterns, fears,
social relationships, attitudes and philosophical disposition, if
that conversion is to make a lasting impact upon the individual
and his community (pp. 3–4).

PSYCHOLOGICAL NEEDS THAT
ARE MET IN THE CHURCH

There are seven concepts that I believe make up the core
of true psychology within the "Black Church." These concepts
are: self-actualization, hope, meaning to life, worldview, a new
creation, identity, and transcendence.

Self-Actualization. Abraham Maslow (1972), a psychologist,
defined the human's highest need as the need for self-actualization.
That is, all that a person can be one must be. Christianity, biblically practiced and exercised, takes the individual to one's
highest level and allows the person to become fully who he or
she is.

The true church allows individuals to become all that one

could become. The true church allowed and allows total development by an individual. In the true church, the individual can develop all dimensions—mind, body, soul, and spirit.

Christian self-actualization differs radically from humanistic self-actualization. Humanistic self-actualization occurs when an individual becomes all that one can be within the context of human standards and parameters. However, Christian self-actualization occurs when one becomes all he or she can become since the Christian's personal development is moderated by and occurs within the context of Jesus Christ and the parameters and principles of Scripture. The Christian becomes self-actualized as movement toward maturity or perfection is occurring. For believers in Christ Jesus, perfection does not mean sinless, but implies growth and movement toward maturity.

Jesus, for example, indicated in Matthew 22:37–40 that for Christians the great commandment in the law is: "Thou shall love the Lord thy God with all thy heart, and with all thy soul, and with all thy mind. This is the first and great commandment. And the second is like unto it, Thou shalt love thy neighbor as thyself. On these two commandments hang all the law and the prophets."

Hence, the self-actualized Christian would express love and have mature relationships on three dimensions: to God, to fellow humanity, and to self. Martin Luther King Jr. aptly suggested that to live a complete life; that is, a self-actualized life, one must be complete on all three dimensions (King, 1998).

Hope. Critical to overcoming a crisis is the ability to have and sustain hope. Frankl (1963) in the book *Man's Search for Meaning* showed how hope was a critical variable for those who survived the Jewish concentration camps.

The historical situation of Blacks in America—mainly one of slavery and oppression—under normal circumstances would

break one's spirit. But Blacks, armed with a hope in and vision
of God and an opportunity to assemble together even under the
rubric of the church as an "invisible institution," were able to
encourage each other and to focus on the true Christian message. This life-giving message is deeply undergirded and sustained by and through hope. Even today one of the favorite
hymns sung in many churches is, "My Hope is Built on Nothing Less than Jesus' Blood and Righteousness." Other historical songs as well as sermons infused with the good news of
Christ were steeped in the element of hope.

In Scripture, the word "hope" is prominent in both the Old
and New Testaments. In the New Testament, hope (Greek *elpis*)
carries the idea of "anticipation with pleasure" or "confidence"
(Strong, 1996). Christian hope is anchored in the promises of
God. The apostle Paul said of hope in Romans 8:24–25: "For
we are saved by hope: but hope that is seen is not hope: for what
a man seeth, why doth he yet hope for? But if we hope for that
we see not, then do we with patience wait for it." In Hebrews
11:1, it is stated: "Now faith is the substance of things hoped
for, the evidence of things not seen." Thus, hope is an element
of faith.

Hope is also a needed element for an enduring life. Those
who decide to live rather than commit suicide often have a high
degree of hope. Hope is still taught in the "Black Church."
Hope, therefore, is an integral part of the true Christian message and is reinforced in healthy church settings. Hope thus has
deep spiritual and psychological meaning and implication. Psychologically, hope may be defined as a belief that leads one to
strive for a certain outcome with the expectation that the outcome will occur.

Meaning to Life. The nature of the Christian message is one
that, when properly understood and applied, gives meaning

to life. The church, with its message of hope and its vision of humankind that are abstracted from a biblical viewpoint, makes a profound impact on the believer. The church and its message actually give new meaning to life. This meaning in turn gives a direction to life.

In Scripture, it was common for people to undergo name changes as they took on new roles. The examples of Abraham, Sarah, and Paul come quickly to mind. In Scripture, when one became a Christian they were viewed differently and given different descriptions, such as, saints, friends, and so on.

Worldview. Every individual has what the German philosophers called a *Weltanschauung*, or a worldview. That is, every individual has a manner in which he or she views the world. This view in turn affects how one operates, what one will and will not do. People have worldviews whether they are conscious of them or not.

Writers have contrasted the Eurocentric worldview with that of an African worldview. This was covered in chapter 2. As noted, the Eurocentric view is individual-oriented while the Afrocentric worldview, in contrast, focuses on cooperation and is group-centered. Representative phrases that capture the African orientation are, "I am, therefore we are" and "It takes a village to raise a child."

One's worldview has a profound impact on one's psychology of life and one's behavior. The "Black Church" teaches a worldview. It is Biblio-centric and views life as important, ordained of God, with a future life that is even better. This "otherworldly" aspect of religion has been misinterpreted by many, including Black writers. Such writers saw the "otherworldliness" as escapism or as "opium of the people." While one must admit that in the practice of Christianity, one can exhibit escapism, true religion/Christianity is both "this and otherworldly." Jesus indi-

cated in His high priestly prayer that we are *"in* the world but
not *of* the world" (see John 17:11–17; italics mine). It is the
proper understanding of this and other Scriptures that allows
one to maintain sanity in the midst of oppression, hatred, discrimination, etc. Without such a view it would have been easy
for our foreparents to give up and say, "What's the use?"

A New Creation. The possibility and reality of becoming
someone new is offered by Jesus Christ when one is placed in
the true church. Second Corinthians 5:17 states: "Therefore if
any man [person] be in Christ, he [or she] is a new creature [cre-
ation]: old things are passed away; behold, all things are become new." This is a profound message of the Gospel and true
church. Imagine slaves who were humiliated and treated as less
than persons but had within them the message of being a new
creation in Christ.

Identity. Similar to the idea of a new creation, true Christianity offers the believer a new or unique identity. Many biblical passages speak to this. For example, the Bible refers to
believers as saints, disciples, a peculiar people, the light of the
world, the salt of the earth, and a royal priesthood, to name a
few. Further, the believer is pictured as having the Holy Spirit
indwelling him/her and sealed by the Spirit of God until the day
of redemption.

There are songs that also portray this idea. For example,
such songs as "I Am a Soldier of the Cross" and "I Am on the
Battlefield for My Lord" convey this new identity.

Transcendence. By transcendence is meant the ability to
remain one's self but to go beyond the self. This ability is a
key element in Christianity. Transcendence occurs when one
views self as possessing more than a physical body; when one
recognizes that he/she is also spirit/soul; when one believes that

there is a life beyond this life. Songs such as "There is a Brighter Day Ahead" and "Higher Ground" capture this idea. Transcendence is experienced when one can feel God's presence during personal or corporate worship.

CONCLUSION

Both the pastor and the church community have been major contributors to promoting the spiritual as well as the psychological well-being of individuals. While the landscape has changed dramatically over the years, both the church setting and the pastor remain vital to the overall well-being of individuals involved in the church community.

It is my belief that the historical "Black Church" had more of a way-of-life effect on its parishioners than many contemporary congregations do. Further, as individuals began to compartmentalize their lives, some of the natural psychological benefits arising from church involvement started to dissipate. As the deep psychological impact of the "Black Church" began to be removed from it, its all-embracing benefits also started to wane.

Although what is called the "Black Church" is still the most powerful institution within the Black community, there is a need for some midcourse corrections. Though there are many encouraging signs, the dangers are there also. Our challenge in the years ahead is to continue to maximize the resources that will advance Christ's church as a whole.

REFERENCES

Frankl, V. (1963). *Man's Search for Meaning: An Introduction to Logotherapy.* New York: Washington Square Press.

Hamilton, C. V. (1972). *The Black Preacher in America.* New York: William Morrow.

Maslow, A. (1972). *The Farther Reaches of Human Nature.* New York: The Viking Press.

Mbiti, J. S. (1970). *African Religions and Philosophy.* Garden City: Anchor Books.

Mitchell, H. (1979). *Black Preaching.* New York: Harper and Row.

Pipes, W. H. (1951). *Say Amen, Brother! Old-Time Negro Preaching: A Study in American Frustration.* New York: The William-Frederick Press.

Strong, J. (1996). *The New Strong's Exhaustive Concordance of the Bible.* Nashville: Thomas Nelson.

Woodson, C. G. (1921). *The History of the Negro Church.* Washington, D.C.: Associated Publishers.

CHAPTER 6

Rituals, Offerings, Songs, and Prayers

"For as often as ye eat this bread, and drink this cup, ye do shew the Lord's death till he come."
1 CORINTHIANS 11:26

"Bring ye all the tithes into the storehouse, that there may be meat in mine house . . ."
MALACHI 3:10

"Every man according as he purposeth in his heart, so let him give; not grudgingly, or of necessity: for God loveth a cheerful giver."
2 CORINTHIANS 9:7

"Come before his presence with singing."
PSALM 100:2

"Men ought always to pray, and not to faint."
LUKE 18:1

INTRODUCTION

Activities that occur within the church and the manner in which they unfold collectively affect, strengthen, and maintain the behavior of its members. These recurring activities will be referenced in this chapter as rituals, offerings, songs, and prayers.

Rituals. Two rituals will be discussed: that of baptism and communion. While both of these have clear biblical sanctions and deep theological significance, the emphasis here is on primarily exploring their psychological dimensions.

Within the "Black Church" and depending on the denomination, the ritual of baptism is performed differently. For some it is done by total immersion and others practice "sprinkling." Some baptize in the name of the Father, Son, and Holy Spirit while others baptize in the name of Jesus only. But regardless of the specific practice, this act has tremendous spiritual and psychological significance to the one being baptized as well as upon the congregation.

In baptism (Matthew 3:16), one experiences identification with Jesus Christ, a movement from being a "sinner" to becoming a "saint." It is a washing away of sins, a cleansing, and is part of becoming a new person in Christ. Participating in baptism does not "save" the person, but it is an act that follows the acceptance of Jesus Christ as one's personal Savior and Lord. It is a public act that identifies the person with Christ and with the congregation, the body of believers. After baptism, the person is typically welcomed and given "the right hand of fellowship." Therefore, the person takes on a new life both in reference to God and in the local congregation of which he or she is a member.

Communion (Matthew 26:26–29), like baptism, is an ordinance that Jesus Christ Himself participated in and is something that is expected of those who believe in Him. In effect, it is to be done in "remembrance of Him." Communion is seen, as stated in 1 Corinthians 11, as an act that commemorates Jesus' broken body and shed blood. Thus individuals who participate or partake of communion are identifying with Jesus Christ and His suffering for the salvation of humankind.

When these rituals, or ordinances, are seriously done and properly understood, they are powerful statements to the persons and congregations involved, as well as an outward sign to nonbelievers that those involved are different. Consequently, participating in them will affect behaviors.

Offerings. While the biblical expectation of giving for believers is carried out through tithes and offerings, many congregations still succumb to other methods of receiving and raising money. Although some of these practices are understandable historically, there seems to be no real justification or rationale for many of the various fund-raising practices that continue. Here I am speaking of such practices as baby contests, the selling of dinners, Tom Thumb weddings, Ms. Church contests, etc. All of these activities seem to have outlived their usefulness as viable fund-raising efforts, particularly as a way to regularly support the congregation. More fundamentally, these practices can bring shame upon the name of Jesus Christ and often communicate to those outside of the congregation that there is a level of spiritual immaturity operating among the members.

How and why, then, do such practices continue and even flourish in some situations? In many ways, they are maintained because the pastor involved usually allows them to be connected with anniversaries or building projects. Thus, to do them is framed as showing honor to the pastor and to being a loyal supporter of the church. The motivation in many churches is each year to raise more money on such days than the last and therefore more gimmicks are employed. Often the men and women are set up to compete with each other and to determine who can raise the most money. Usually, the pastor verbally reinforces these efforts. Visiting pastors who speak at such events, particularly pastors' anniversaries, often praise the congregation on their showing of "love" that is typically equated with the amount of money raised and the elaborateness of the ceremony.

Another practice in many congregations is to have the congregation walk around the table when giving. I have seen this practiced in a "healthy" manner as well as in a manipulative way. Many times, in both instances, the words "you can't beat God giving, no matter how hard you try" are sung. While there is nothing in and of itself wrong with this exercise, it is sometimes used as a tactic for inducing guilt. Those who may not have normally given in the offering do not refrain because they are "put on the spot" through this procedure.

Additionally, at offering time the technique of announcing amounts is used. Sometimes the appeal is for people to match the pastor in giving a certain amount that is stated from the pulpit. Thus, the "real" Christian is the one who can match the pastor. Another technique is to ask for a certain amount based on one's "status" in the church. For example, pastors may be asked to give one amount, "ministers" another, deacons another, and so on.

127

All of these, while they may be effective in securing the desired offering, violate basic scriptural principles and more than often induce guilt.

Songs. There is found in some songs a deep religious, psychological, emotional, spiritual, and theological significance. The songs sung in "Black churches" often speak of a brighter day, assurance, hope, being on the battlefield, heaven, victory, and the power of God. Many observers of religion and gospel singing will admit that few sing with such creativity, melody, fervor, and emotion as Black people.

One of the earliest known treatments of the importance and role of songs in the development and survival of Black people was done by DuBois (1961). His essay that appeared in the book *The Souls of Black Folk* (originally published in 1903) was titled "Of the Sorrow Songs." On this contribution and unique art form, DuBois stated:

> Little of beauty has America given the world save the rude grandeur God himself stamped on her bosom; the human spirit in this new world has expressed itself in vigor and ingenuity rather than in beauty. And so by fateful chance the Negro folksong—the rhythmic cry of the slave—stands today, not simply as the sole American music, but as the most beautiful expression of human experience born this side of the seas. It has been neglected, it has been, and is, half despised, and above all it has been persistently mistaken and misunderstood; but notwithstanding, it still remains as the singular spiritual heritage of the nation and the greatest gift of the Negro people (pp.181–182).

DuBois, using his great intellect and scholarly background, did an excellent job of stating the significance of these songs to the "psychology" of Black survival. Speaking directly to this issue, he stated:

> What are these songs, and what do they mean? I know little of music and can say nothing in technical phrase, but I know something of men, and knowing them, I know that these songs are the articulate message of the slave to the world. They tell us in these eager days that life was joyous to the black slave, careless and happy. I can easily believe this of some, of many. But not all the past South, though it rose from the dead, can gainsay the heart-touching witness of these songs. They are the music of an unhappy people, of the children of disappointment; they tell of death and suffering and unvoiced longing toward a truer world, of misty wanderings and hidden ways (p. 183).

DuBois further stated:

> Through all the sorrow of the Sorrow Songs there breathes a hope—a faith in the ultimate justice of things. The minor cadences of despair change often to triumph and calm confidence. Sometimes it is faith in life, sometimes a faith in death, sometimes assurance of boundless justice in some fair world beyond. But whichever it is, the meaning is always clear: that sometime, somewhere, men will judge men by their souls and not by their skins. Is such a hope justified? Do the Sorrow Songs sing true? (p. 189).

Cone (1972) in the book *The Spirituals and the Blues* also did a treatise of the role of songs in and on the lives, identity, and survival of Black people. In the Introduction of his book, he stated:

> Black music is a living reality . . . Black music is also social and political. It is social because it is *black* and thus articulates the

separateness of the black community. It is an artistic rebellion
against the humiliating deadness of western culture. Black music is political because in it is the rejection of the white cultural
values, it affirms the political "otherness" of black people.
Through song, a new political consciousness is continuously
created, one antithetical to the laws of white society . . . Black
music is also theological. That is, it tells us about the divine
Spirit that moves the people toward unity and self-determination.
It is not possible to be black and encounter the Spirit of black
emotion and not be moved. My purpose is to uncover the theological presuppositions of black music as reflected in the spirituals and the blues, asking: What do they tell us about black
people's deepest aspiration and devotion? I will ask questions
about God, Jesus Christ, life after death, and suffering; and I
will seek to investigate these in the light of black people's historical strivings for freedom (pp. 6–7).

The reader is encouraged to consult Cone's work to see in detail the power and theology of the spirituals.

Wyatt Tee Walker (1979) has also written regarding Black
sacred music in the book *Somebody's Calling My Name: Black
Sacred Music and Social Change*. This is a very valuable work
in that it looks at the history of Blacks in reference to music.
The book also discusses the overall importance of music to
the "Black Church." In this regard, a statement by Walker is
worth noting:

Music is one of the three major support systems in Black
Church worship. Preaching and praying are the other two. It is
difficult to conclusively say which is the most important. After
the act of the emancipation in 1865, preaching became central
and remains so today. However, the characteristics of authentic
Black preaching have been so heavily influenced by the charac-

teristics of Black sacred music that a strong argument could be advanced to establish that singing is of equal importance. Let it suffice to submit that preaching is central, with a clear footnote that singing is a very close second. The fact is that most ministers follow a tradition of singing or attempting to sing and that any preacher who sings acceptably has a decided edge on the preacher that does not sing at all. Again, the dominance of worship time—singing versus preaching—could very well be a toss-up in almost any Black worship experience (p. 22).

What Walker also pointed out in his treatise of music within the Black tradition is how music is critical to the emotions and emotional experience within the "Black Church" and the worship experience.

Prayers. Prayer is communication with God. Within church settings one often hears the comment that he or she "really prayed." Such a comment is made in reference to the emotion and fervor of the prayer more so than to its content.

There is the belief that Black people also developed a unique praying style. This tradition is examined in the book *The Prayer Tradition of Black People* by Carter (1977). According to Carter, there are many functions of prayer. In a chapter titled "Major Functions of the Black Prayer Tradition," Carter acknowledges the otherworldly aspect of the prayers but also articulates other outcomes from these prayers and old-fashioned prayer meetings, such as:

- breeding ground for churches
- training ground for church leaders
- community prayer bands
- female leadership
- a healing ground for physical, mental, and spiritual diseases

131

- warming up for worship
- the old-fashioned mourners' bench
- altar call and blessing line
- bargaining with God for game and gain
- praying the old year out and the new year in
- the altar call; institutionalized church

In subsequent chapters, he listed other functions:

- purification and inner release
- prayer as song and inner release
- a way of making it through life
- as a weapon of social change (liberation and non-violence)

A more recent and research-oriented look at prayer, specifically as a source of coping, is provided by Taylor, Chatters, and Levin (2004). Two distinct patterns of prayer were found: those who prayed in response to particular problems encountered and those for whom prayer was done frequently, intensely, and as an integral part of their lives. Praying was found to be employed for a variety of problems: job issues, health concerns, the need for strength, stress, worry, and so on.

CONCLUSION

Rituals, offerings, songs, and prayers are all vital in the life of a church community. The rituals of baptism and communion, as well as prayer, have clear biblical sanctions. Songs, likewise, are critical to worship. The challenge is to continue these practices in a manner that is consistent with Scripture.

REFERENCES

Carter, H. A. (1977). *The Prayer Tradition of Black People*. Valley Forge: Judson.

Cone, J. (1972). *The Spirituals and the Blues*. New York: Seabury.

DuBois, W. E. B. (1961). *The Souls of Black Folks*. New York: Fawcett.

Taylor, R. J., L. M. Chatters, and J. Levin (2004). *Religion in the Lives of African Americans—Social, Psychological, and Health Perspectives*. Thousands Oaks: Sage Publications.

Walker, W. T. (1979). *Somebody's Calling My Name—Black Sacred Music and Social Change*. Valley Forge: Judson.

CHAPTER 7

Innocent but Potentially Detrimental Statements, Concepts, and Beliefs

"For as he thinketh in his heart, so is he . . ."
PROVERBS 23:7

"Wherefore, my beloved brethren, let every man be swift to hear, slow to speak, slow to wrath."
JAMES 1:19

INTRODUCTION

This chapter draws on my many years of hearing statements within the church setting that are made in the fervor of a sermon, in a testimony, in a song, or in a talk. Such statements are typically offered in a genuine manner and are assumed to be accurate and/or are expressed in order to demonstrate that one has a deep relationship with God. Within a church setting, these phrases can also suggest that the church service is one that is "powerful" and/or pleasing to God. Below, I will examine these statements and show how they may be uttered innocently. Additionally, I will discuss why and how these statements are or may have the potential to be psychologically damaging or detrimental because they are inconsistent with Scripture. Later in this chapter, I will expand the discussion to cover the concept of "toxic faith" and conclude with what needs to be done to prevent the ill effects of erroneous ideas and beliefs that are taken outside of a biblical context.

THE STATEMENTS AND/OR PHRASES

Below, I will discuss seven of these statements/phrases that are commonly used in some church settings.

"Anything dead needs to be buried."
Devotion leaders or speakers often make this statement when they seek to "liven up" the church service. Such a statement is intended to get the people more involved and outwardly expressive by doing the following: "saying amen," singing, clapping, standing, shouting, and so on.

This statement is innocent in the sense that the person who utters it is typically sincere and truly desires to get people involved in the worship experience and to express themselves physically. The statement, however, can be detrimental because it equates emotions with spirituality and worshiping. It is further potentially detrimental because it does not allow for the individuality or diversity of worship expressions. Some people are more reserved when it comes to emotions and still others feel deeply but do not express it outwardly. Some express themselves by meditating; others do so by crying and some by silently reflecting on and worshiping God. Such a statement also can rob, or at least interfere with, an individual who might want to quietly worship and meditate.

"If you have Jesus, you don't need anything else" or "I got Jesus and that's enough."
The above descriptions are generic ways in which this thought is expressed. The statement itself is uttered in a variety of contexts and settings. For example, it may be made in reference to the use of counseling or psychiatric services, the use of medicines, the use of physicians, etc. It may be uttered innocently because the one who utters it actually believes or wants to con-

vey the biblical idea of the all-encompassing sufficiency of God, His omnipotence and superiority above all humanity and human methods. The person who utters it may want to show his or her dependence on Jesus Christ and may be reflecting his or her personal situation or experience. However, these phrases can have damaging consequences for other people.

For example, I have heard this comment or variants of it made in situations wherein I have personally known people in the audience or congregation who are Christians (that is, have accepted Jesus Christ as their personal Savior and Lord) but are themselves in a counseling relationship or are using various medications. The net effect often on the person in such a situation is to feel that they are not "Christian enough" and may result in the person's feeling guilty or lead them to further devalue themselves and possibly question their relationship with God. Such a statement fails to understand and appreciate that healing takes place in a variety of ways and through a variety of methods. Jesus never condemns the use of such aids. Jesus tells us to "love the Lord thy God with all thy heart, and with all thy soul, and with all thy mind . . . and . . . thy neighbour as thyself" (Matthew 22:37–38). Thus God expects us to be in relationship with Him as well as others.

There is also a song that is still sung which also conveys, at one level, this thought. The song is, "I Got Jesus and That's Enough." While I understand the deeper meaning of this song, it can be interpreted in two ways. The first way of interpretation (the positive way) is that when everything is considered, having Jesus Christ is the most important possession. This interpretation would be consistent with the Scripture wherein we are told to love God, other humanity, and the self. However, the second way of interpretation (the negative way) is problematic when one takes it to mean that other humanity and the self is not important.

"I'd rather have Jesus than silver or gold."

While these words are from a song, they are often uttered in other contexts and can have both a positive and negative meaning. The negative side of the statement exemplifies itself when one desires to show how special their relationship with Jesus Christ is and/or their dependence on Him. This desire is admirable. However, many times when the person utters these words, he or she is simultaneously flashing a gold watch or ring or is wearing a gold or silver necklace or arm bracelet. The person may also be driving a luxury automobile and have an expensive house.

This statement can be detrimental when one does not see the contradiction in what one is saying and modeling. It can thus convey bad theology and suggest to the believer who is not well-grounded or mature to believe or feel that material possessions are in and of themselves bad, or it can imply that the Bible is totally against riches. While Jesus warned against riches, He did not reject riches (silver and gold) outright.

"When praises go up, blessings come down."

This phrase has become increasingly popular. The possible innocent aspect of the statement is that praises can in certain contexts lead to blessings. Usually the phrase is uttered near the conclusion of a sermon or during a devotional service. The intent of the statement is to elicit more outward expressions of praises from the individuals in attendance. It is often uttered in situations that also elicit the earlier statement "anything dead ought to be buried."

The detrimental aspect of the statement is that it can lead a person to believe that the only way to receive "blessings" is through praise. Biblically speaking, praises properly uttered can and do lead to blessings. The other potential detrimental aspect of this phrase is that it ignores the fact that "blessings" can come from various sources. For example, blessings can result from walking upright (Psalms 1) and from tithing (Malachi 3), just to name two instances. The statement further ignores the reality that the nonbeliever also reaps some form of blessings. For in Matthew 5:45 it is stated that ". . . he maketh his sun to rise on the evil and on the good, and sendeth rain on the just and on the unjust."

"Let's have a little church/Let's go churching."

This statement is often made when the desire is to create a certain atmosphere during a church service. It can also be expressed when there is a feeling that the service is not one in which the atmosphere is conducive or representative of a certain style of worship. This sentiment is also representative of a song that is sometimes sung by choirs and congregations. The statement is an "innocent" one in the sense that the choir or congregation often is unaware that the message conveyed is inaccurate biblically. One who utters such phrases probably believes that the atmosphere that is created determines "church." The message that is communicated is damaging because it leads one to believe that "having church" is determined by the content of a service. Nothing could be further from the truth. Nowhere in Scripture are we told to "have church" or to "go churching." The Bible is clear in asserting that believers are the church. Those who utter such phrases and congregations that allow such phrases to be spoken and songs to be sung are demonstrating their lack of sound biblical theology on this matter.

I have been in several services where the phrases have been uttered and the song has been sung. It is sad to observe that when this occurs, many in the congregation will say "amen" in response to those conveyances. I have even observed pastors and "ministers" doing the same thing, with seemingly little awareness of what they are doing.

"Get your praise on"/"Praise is what I do."

Either of these statements can be very detrimental. They are both borrowed from the "secular" world. Remember the statements "get your groove on" and "love is what I do." While God desires praise, attempting to praise without the proper attitude is rejected (see Amos 5:23). The most detrimental aspect of speaking or singing these phrases is that they often isolate praise from an overall lifestyle and can lead people to believe that they can please God simply by "praising."

"You can't beat God giving, no matter how hard you try."

This is part of a song and is usually sung or uttered during the offering. While the phrase above is accurate, what follows these words is problematic. After the phrase "you can't beat God giving," next comes "the more you give, the more He gives to you." The detrimental aspect of this phrase is that it suggests, equates, and correlates a financial return from giving. Thus individuals may develop the wrong motive for giving.

THE ISSUE OF TOXIC FAITH

There is a growing body of writing and research that deals with the issue of healthy and unhealthy religion, or toxic faith. The use of statements such as the ones discussed above may be indicative of a deeper problem within congregations—that is, the practice and presence of toxic faith.

Stephen Arterburn and Jack Felton (2001) in the book *Toxic Faith* defined toxic faith as: "a destructive and dangerous involvement in a religion that allows the religion, not a relationship with God, to control a person's life" (p. 19). Arterburn and Felton list the following twenty-one beliefs of a toxic faith:

• God's love and favor depend on my behavior

- When tragedy strikes, true believers should have a real peace about it
- If I have real faith, God will heal me or someone I am praying for
- All ministers are men and women of God and can be trusted
- Material blessings are a sign of spiritual strength
- The more money I give to God, the more money He will give to me
- I can work my way to heaven
- Problems in my life result from some particular sin
- I must not stop meeting others' needs
- I must always submit to authority
- God uses only spiritual giants
- Having true faith means waiting for God to help me and doing nothing until He does
- If it's not in the Bible, it isn't relevant
- God will find me a perfect mate
- Everything that happens to me is good
- A strong faith will protect me from problems and pain
- God hates sinners, is angry with me, and wants to punish me
- Christ was merely a good teacher
- God is too big to care about me
- More than anything else, God wants me to be happy
- I can become God

In a similar book to *Toxic Faith*, Cloud and Townsend (1995) in *12 "Christian" Beliefs that Can Drive You Crazy* presented and discussed these beliefs and their origins. They stated that their patients were handicapped by certain teachings that sounded like, but were not, genuine Christian beliefs. These twelve ideas (assumptions) are:

- It's selfish to have my needs met
- If I'm spiritual enough, I will have no pain or suffering
- If I change my behavior, I will grow spiritually and emotionally
- I just need to give "it" to the Lord
- One day, I'll be finished with recovery
- Leave the past behind
- If I have God, I don't need people
- "Shoulds" are good
- Guilt and shame are good for me
- If I make right choices, I will grow spiritually
- Just doing the right thing is more important than why I do it
- If I know the truth, I will grow

Regarding these twelve ideas, Cloud and Townsend indicate that:

> The ideas appeared true because those who taught them used religious language and quoted Scriptures. These ideas, however, are emotional heresies. They are false assumptions about spiritual and emotional growth. They aren't biblical, and they don't work.
>
> We identified twelve teachings that sound plausible because they each contain a nugget of truth. At some point, however, when Christians try to apply these truths, a breakdown occurs. And the person needlessly suffers (p. 9).

Cloud and Townsend further state that "most of these false assumptions have one thing in common: They draw the believer away from God's resources of growth and healing, and toward a system that sounds Christian, but doesn't work" (p. 10).

CONCLUSION
WHAT NEEDS TO BE DONE IN REFERENCE
TO THESE STATEMENTS AND TOXIC FAITH

As can be seen from just a cursory review, erroneous ideas and beliefs can abound throughout church and religious communities. However, we must strive to be true to the Scriptures and thereby create a psychologically healthy environment that is consistent with the Word of God. To do so, we need to exercise greater caution before using such statements or singing certain songs that convey these potentially damaging meanings. If these phrases are to be used or if these songs are to be sung, we need to explain more fully what is meant when the phrases are uttered or we need to better contextualize them. While it is true that "Christ is All," it is also true that God still works within the context of humanity and its abundant resources.

For example, in the following scriptural accounts, Elisha told Naaman to go and wash seven times in the Jordan to receive his healing (2 Kings 5:10). During the process of healing blindness, Jesus spat on the ground, applied the clay to someone's eyes, and told the man to go and wash in the pool of Siloam (John 9:6–7). The apostle Paul sought God three times to remove the thorn in his flesh, yet God chose not to do so (2 Corinthians 12:7–9). Thus, neither the absence nor presence of problems (psychological or otherwise) is necessarily a sign of deep Christian faith or the lack thereof. The experience of the biblical Job is one example that vividly points this out.

Therefore, it is *extremely critical* that congregations examine their practices and beliefs to make sure that they are not creating, practicing, or reinforcing a toxic faith system. We must carefully examine our statements and belief system to make certain that we do not "have a zeal for God, but not according to knowledge" (Romans 10:2).

REFERENCES

Arterburn, S. and J. Felton (2001). *Toxic Faith: Experiencing Healing from Painful Spiritual Abuse.* Colorado Springs: WaterBrook Press.

Cloud, H. and J. Townsend (1995). *12 "Christian" Beliefs that Can Drive You Crazy: Relief from False Assumptions.* Grand Rapids: Zondervan.

PART 4
COUNSELING AND PSYCHOLOGICAL SERVICE DELIVERY

Psychotherapy
(Mental Health Counseling)
and the Church

■

Counseling in
the Religious Arena—
The Potentials and Challenges

CHAPTER 8

Psychotherapy (Mental Health Counseling) and the Church*

"And his name shall be called Wonderful, Counsellor, The mighty God, The everlasting Father, The Prince of Peace."

ISAIAH 9:6

▪

"Where no counsel is, the people fall: but in the multitude of counsellors there is safety."

PROVERBS 11:14

---

*This chapter is a further elaboration and update of a paper originally presented at the International Congress on Christian Counseling in Atlanta, GA on November 9–13, 1988.

INTRODUCTION

In the preceding chapters, it has been shown and discussed how the elements of psychology operate within various aspects and segments of the church. In this and the next chapter, I will discuss in greater detail the field and profession of psychology, counseling, and psychotherapy and their relationship to and possibilities within the church. Specifically, how formal psychotherapy and mental health counseling are viewed and practiced within the church community and the "Black Church" in particular will be examined.

In doing so, the following areas will be covered:

1. Historical and contemporary emphases of the "Black Church"
2. Psychological services and the Black community—implications for the "Black Church"
3. Perceptions by the "Black Church" community in regard to psychological services and counseling
4. Suggestions and needed directions in regard to professional counseling and the church

Historical Emphases of
the "Black Church"

What have been the historical emphases in "Black churches," and where have psychological and mental health services fit in the picture? I will answer this question by examining the writings of DuBois, Woodson, Mays and Nicholson, and Lincoln and Mamiya.

DuBois (1899) in the classic study titled "The Philadelphia Negro" examined "Black churches" in Philadelphia, Pennsylvania, around the end of the 19th century. In this study he described six functions. Listed in order of emphasis were:

- the raising of the annual budget
- the maintenance of membership
- social intercourse and amusements
- the setting of moral standards
- promotion of general intelligence
- efforts for social betterment (p. 202)

DuBois was careful to note that even though moral standards were listed fourth, this did not imply that Blacks and the churches were hypocritical or irreligious. Rather, the priorities reflected the need in the churches under study for an adequate budget to assure organizational survival. In the list and given the date of the study (late 1800s), the status of psychology and counseling within the Black community and the larger society during this time period, it is not surprising to see no reference to counseling type services.

While Woodson (1921) did not do a specific listing of activities/functions as did DuBois, he did mention various activities within the church setting throughout his book such as preaching, education, employment, social welfare, etc. The fol-

148

lowing statements by Woodson implied who was responsible for "psychotherapy" within the "Black Church":

> The ministry is more attractive among Negroes than among whites. The White minister has only one important function to perform in his group, that of spiritual leadership. To the Negro community the preacher is this and besides the walking encyclopedia, the *counselor* of the unwise, the friend of the unfortunate, the *social welfare organizer*, and the interpreter of the signs of the times. No man is properly introduced to the Negro community unless he comes through the minister, and no movement can expect success there unless it has his cooperation or endorsement (p. 257; italics mine).

Mays and Nicholson (1933), some thirty years after DuBois and about a decade after Woodson, reported on the frequency of forty activities within 609 urban churches. Their study showed that preaching, union services and interchurch cooperation, missionary societies, and clubs (education, social, and financial) were in all churches. Sunday schools were in 608 (99.8%); poor relief was in 590 (96.9%); revivals were present in 561 (92.1%); choirs were in 503 (82.6%); young people's work in 398 (65.4%); prayer meetings in 388 (63.7%); recreational work was in 191 (31.4%); and pastors' aid boards were in 77 (12.6%). The other activities were at frequencies less than 10%.

Activities that seemed somewhat related to psychological and counseling services were represented at the following frequencies and percentages: free clinic–5 (.8%); visiting nurse–2 (.3%); and health classes–1 (.2%). Thus with the passage of time we see a slight emerging presence of counseling type services.

Almost eighty years after DuBois' study and some fifty years after Mays and Nicholson, Lincoln and Mamiya's (1990) study (survey actually conducted in 1983) showed that there was cooperation between rural and urban churches and social agencies that dealt with drug and alcohol abuse cases and those that dealt with health-related problems. The percent of cooperation by these rural churches was 0.6% and 0.8%, respectively.

As to their study of urban churches and pastoral responsibility, Lincoln and Mamiya (1990) found that visitation and counseling ranked fifth among nine categories in order of importance. Preaching was ranked first and teaching second. They also found that 95 (4.4%) of the total churches studied in one sample cooperated with drug and alcohol abuse agencies and programs.

The writings by DuBois and Mays and Nicholson clearly suggest that mental health type counseling services beyond what the pastor provided were not present in very visible ways. Rather, the "Black Church" historically focused on survival issues, the saving of souls, the transmission of a culture, education, social needs, and a place of refuge and rallying for an oppressed people. Psychological needs were met within that context. However, in Lincoln and Mamiya's study, one sees some slight movement toward issues related to psychological and mental health matters.

Given the above, it would seem that "Black churches" in the latter half of the 20th century and in the early 21st century would be more open to counseling and psychological services and have them as part of their activities. This assertion will be explored in a later section titled "Suggestions and Needed Direction in Regard to Counseling and the "Black Church." However, first I present some of the research on the perceptions of mental health and counseling services.

PERCEPTIONS BY THE "BLACK CHURCH" COMMUNITY IN REGARD TO MENTAL HEALTH PROFESSIONALS AND COUNSELING SERVICES

How do "Black congregations" and parishioners view mental health issues, services, and practitioners? Richardson (1981) assessed the attitudes of Black clergy (pastors) and parishioners toward mental illness and mental health professionals. His sample consisted of twenty-seven pastors and eighty-one parishioners —thus representing 84% of the "Black churches" in a midwestern city. Various denominations were included. Particularly germane to the topic under consideration is the finding regarding the pastors' and parishioners' attitudes toward mental health professionals.

Using the semantic differential technique and the scales: "sincere-insincere," "valuable-worthless," "wise-foolish," "safe-dangerous," "dependable-undependable," "relaxed-tense," and "clean-dirty" against the stimulus categories: psychiatrist, psychologist, and counselor, Richardson (1981) found favorable attitudes on the part of both parishioners and clergy. On a seven-point scale, the overall mean responses for pastors were: 5.96 for the psychiatrist; 5.90 for the psychologist; and 5.75 for the counselor. Across the scales, the parishioners' mean values were: psychiatrist 5.29; psychologist 5.36; and counselor 4.48.

The Richardson study further showed that even though both the pastors and parishioners held favorable attitudes toward mental health professionals, the pastors held a statistically significant more favorable attitude toward the psychiatrist and psychologist than did parishioners.

Solomon (1985) reported on the results of a demonstration project funded by the National Institute of Mental Health. The project was designed to train inner-city ministers in California in regard to mental health issues (including the referral process) and to develop a model of collaboration between a family counseling agency and the "Black Church."

Three church sites were selected (Pentecostal, Baptist, and United Methodist). One counselor staffed each site. Each site was connected by telephone and one of the sites housed the overall coordinator and the project's administrative secretary. The project had an advisory committee consisting of ministers, laypersons, and representatives from key community agencies. It was in existence for two and one-half years and was open to the broader community.

The project received approximately 775 referrals. Of these, 31% were from church-related sources (6% were from ministers and 25% from church organizations). It was further found that 47% of the church-referred clients had not received counseling before. Solomon (1985) further compared the clients who had received services from the church-based program only with those who also had received counseling from another agency for the same or different problems. Statistically, she found that those who had used only the church-based counseling reported significantly more favorable attitudes regarding those services.

Overall, the data suggested that the program was successful in increasing referrals and had a positive impact on the community. Solomon felt that it was successful because it was offered in a church-based rather than a traditional site. Thus this represents one model for enhancing the perceptions toward counseling in the Black community. Throughout the project, it seems that the attitudes within the community toward the services were positive.

During the mid-1980s, I surveyed ten persons from different congregations in churches throughout the country via telephone interviews. This was done in an effort to assess attitudes toward counseling and mental health services in the church environment, the extent to which counseling programs were in existence, and the type of activities in which the churches were typically engaged. The results reflect opinions of persons residing in the states of Georgia, Pennsylvania, California, Connecticut, Mississippi, Michigan, Illinois, and Washington, D.C. The participants were chosen because they represented geographical diversity and were knowledgeable of "Black Church" issues and activities.

The results of the survey may be summarized as follows:

- Three of the churches (30%) reported having a formal counseling program or a mental health center within its premises. A formal program was defined as a staff of counselors who offered services in a predictable manner.
- The three counseling programs had been in existence for three, twelve, and seven years, respectively.
- As to why the other churches didn't have counseling programs, the primary reasons given were:
  a. The minister is viewed as the person who would counsel.
  b. The church's budget would not permit it.
  c. The personnel are not available.
  d. The lack of support and adequate space.
- As to the respondents' personal attitudes regarding the value of psychological counseling, one saw it as of no value, two viewed it to have some value, and seven viewed it as having great value.
- Seven of the respondents were not aware of other predominantly "Black churches" in their city having counseling programs.
- As to their personal attitude toward Christians receiving psychological counseling, two were unfavorable, one was somewhat favorable, and seven were very favorable.

Hence, 80% were favorable toward Christians receiving counseling of a psychological nature.

- Regarding the respondents' perceptions of the general attitude in the "Black Church" toward mental health counseling, the responses were varied. That is, two indicated unfavorable, two somewhat unfavorable, two favorable, three somewhat favorable, and one very favorable.

- In response to the question regarding whether their churches offered workshops, seminars, institutes, etc., all ten answered in the affirmative.

- The types of seminars, workshops, and institutes offered were varied. Those mentioned were: Christian education, premarital issues, discipleship, marriage issues, finances, being single, men issues, women issues, parenting, male-female relationships, family issues, job seminars, youth issues, career fairs, health issues, academic enrichment programs, spiritual enrichment, and rape issues.

- In reference to the question regarding how often workshops are offered within the broader "Black Church" community, one responded very infrequently, five infrequently, and four frequently.

Though this survey is small and has some methodological inadequacies, it provides some interesting glimpses into the evolving more positive attitudes of Black Christians toward the field of counseling and mental health services.

Taylor, Ellison, Chatters, Levin, and Lincoln (2000) reported that approximately 18% of church-based programs involved some form of counseling and intervention for community members.

Mamiya (2006) reported that from a survey of Black pastors

done by the ITC/Faith Factor Project 2000 reflecting a range of denominations, 66% said that their congregations provided counseling services or "hotlines" and 52% provided substance abuse programs.

These results collectively are encouraging and need to be further developed. The next section will offer suggestions as to how this might be done.

SUGGESTIONS AND NEEDED DIRECTION IN REGARD TO COUNSELING AND THE "BLACK CHURCH"

Given the increasingly favorable attitudes of pastors and parishioners toward mental health professionals in the Richardson study (1981), the success of the Solomon project (1985), the overall favorable attitudes toward counseling found in the survey conducted by me, and the results noted in the Taylor et al. study (2000), several suggestions can be made as to how to enhance the use of counseling and counseling resources within the "Black Church."

First, Richardson (1981, 1989) offered the following:

- Mental health agencies must employ the Black clergy as consultants and chaplains.
- Educational institutions should establish consultation relationships with the clergy. As such, educational institutions could make use of the skills of the clergy in the formal training programs for mental health professionals.
- Educational institutions should conduct periodic seminars for the Black clergy on the latest developments in the mental health field.

Implementation of the first of Richardson's recommendations would mean that there must be developed a mechanism for both the mental health agencies and the clergy to mutually profit from each other's skills and to learn from each other.

The implementation of the second and third recommendations would allow skill building on the part of trainees and clergy from a formal educational standpoint. Hence, these recommendations challenge those who are in mental health agencies and educational institutions to build bridges with the Black Christian community.

In addition to the above, the following could be done to enhance counseling services for the "Black Church" community.

- Persons who are members of the "Black Church" and have mental health counseling skills must offer themselves as members with skills in contrast to a professional with skills. The distinction between the two is that the church is more likely to use the services of a person as a member who is a professional. Conversely, the church is more likely to be "turned off" by the one who is trying to gain acceptance purely on the basis of being a professional.
- Persons who are members and nonmembers must offer their mental health counseling skills within existing programs. My survey, as well as the Taylor, et. al., (2000) article showed that there are numerous seminars, workshops, and institutes that are *already* a part of the "Black Church" setting that are "psychological" in nature. There is an acceptance by the "Black Church" community to psychologically oriented programs when the clergy can see that there is benefit to the congregation and that the providers understand and respect the nature and purpose of the church.
- Persons who are members of the "Black Church" and have skills in the area must be willing to develop work-

shops, etc., that deal with critical mental health issues.

- Persons interested in enhancing the use of counseling services within the "Black Church" community must understand that there is some tension with the "Black Church" regarding the value of "nonbiblical" counseling. As the earlier survey showed, there are some who question the value of mental health counseling. However, as one looks deeply at the underlying reasons, it seems that it is mainly out of the desire to be assured that the counseling done is biblically based or, at least, respectful of Christian belief. Thus, it behooves the Christian mental health professional to understand the Scriptures and learn how to counsel within a biblical framework. This challenge is true within the entire Christian community and will be explored in the next chapter.

- Mental health professionals must present themselves to pastors and the church as resources. This can be done through developing liaisons with ministerial alliances.

- Black Christian mental health professionals must take on the challenge of establishing formal counseling programs with "Black churches." There is, in many cases, an opening for this to be done.

Critical to reaching Blacks (and others) with counseling services in a church setting is the use of a seeking modality; that is, aggressive outreach. June (1986) outlined and discussed eight factors that agencies and providers need to do in order to reach Black men. These factors are also applicable to the broader population. In that article, I listed the following:

- use a seeking mode as a viable part of service delivery
- staff agencies with a diversity of professionals

- use an aggressive outreach approach
- look for ways to destigmatize the counseling process
- make use of Black psychology (for others, culturally relevant approaches)
- develop relationships with agencies and organizations that are closely connected to this population
- make a distinction between presence of staff and programming to a population
- seek innovative ways to deliver services

Richardson and June (2005) offered the following in reference to maximizing the use of such services within the Christian church context:

- earn acceptance
- explore personal beliefs
- develop a relationship with pastors
- establish and maintain a relationship with local churches
- become acquainted with the religious tradition of the local church or denomination
- become acquainted with the field of biblical counseling
- develop and nurture a collaborative research program

Psychotherapy in "African American churches" has also been discussed by Cook and Wiley (2000). A particular focus of their work is on aspects of the church that may influence the mental health of individuals who attend. Such areas are denominational diversity, community fellowship, role of women, worship practices, role of pastor, grief, and racial liberation. The reader is referred to them for the suggestions they have made in this regard.

A strength-based approach regarding mental health in reference to the "Black Church" has been discussed by Harley (2005).

During the latter part of the 20th century, numerous activities occurred which have made counseling services more acceptable to the church community. Among these are the increased number of Black mental health professionals, the development of culturally sensitive theories and instruments, and the development of Black-oriented mental health organizations (for example, the Association of Black Psychologists, the Association of Multicultural Counseling and Development, the National Association of Biblical Counseling, and the Black African American Christian Counselors).

CONCLUSION

The main conclusion to be drawn from this chapter is that the institutional church and the provision of psychological services need not be antagonists. The "Black Church" (as are all churches) is increasingly open to mental health services delivered in a culturally sensitive manner and with a respect for what the Christian church stands for. Thus, as more Black mental health professionals who are Christians are trained, as all professionals are trained in a more culturally sensitive manner, and as congregations open their own counseling services on-site, one will see even greater acceptance of counseling and psychotherapy within both the "Black Church," the Black community, and the church community in general.

Massey and McKinney (1976) made these observations many years ago in regard to the "Black Church":

The church must, however, put to work the vast variety of skills and expertise residual in the laity. The

159

laity is blessed with so many skills today that it behooves a sensitive congregation to build a "skills bank" so that all the members can be involved in meaningful activities . . . What are some of the opportunities beyond the traditional? (p. 99).

Delivery of health services presents the church with opportunities to use its facilities to provide its constituents and community with the full range of medical, dental, and *psychological* benefits needed in a fast-paced society.

While the church must open its doors to serve people, it must be selective as to who it will let use its facilities. A church should develop guidelines spelling out in no uncertain terms how its facilities will be used, at the same time making clear its commitments to relevant ministry (p. 101; italics mine).

Massey and McKinney's comments are still relevant. The harvest truly is ripe, but the workers must be willing to come forth.

REFERENCES

Cook, D. A. and C. Y. Wiley (2000). *Psychotherapy with Members of African American Churches and Spiritual Traditions.* In Richards, P. S. and A. E. Bergin (Editors). *Handbook of Psychotherapy and Religious Diversity.* Washington, D.C.: American Psychological Association.

DuBois, W. E. B. (1899). *The Philadelphia Negro: A Social Study.* Philadelphia: University of Pennsylvania Press.

Harley, D. A. (2005). *The Black Church: A Strength-Based Approach in Mental Health,* pp. 191–203. In Harley, D. A. and J. M. Dillard (Editors). *Contemporary Mental Health Issues Among African Americans.* Alexandria: American Counseling Association.

June, L. N. (1986). "Enhancing the delivery of mental health and counseling services to Black males: Critical agency and provider responsibilities." *Journal of Multicultural Counseling and Development.* 14, 39–45.

Lincoln, C. E. and L. H. Mamiya (1990). *The Black Church in the African American Experience.* Durham: Duke University Press.

Mamiya, L. (2006). *Pulpit & Pew—Research on Pastoral Leadership. River of Struggle, River of Freedom—Trends Among Black Churches and Black Pastoral Leadership* (Pulpit Research Reports). Durham: Duke Divinity School (www.pulpitandpew.duke.edu).

Massey, F. Jr., and S. B. McKinney (1976). *Church Administration in the Black Perspective.* Valley Forge: Judson.

Mays, B. E. and J. W. Nicholson (1933). *The Negro's Church.* New York: Negroes Universities Press.

Richardson, B. L. (1981). "The attitudes of Black clergy and parishioners toward mental illness and mental health professionals." Unpublished doctoral dissertation, Michigan State University, East Lansing, MI.

_____ (1989). "Attitudes of Black clergy toward mental health professionals: Implications for pastoral care." *Journal of Pastoral Care*. 43, 33–39.

Richardson, B. L. and L. N. June (2005). *Developing Effective Partnerships in Order to Utilize and Maximize the Resources of the African American Church—Strategies and Tools for Counseling Professionals*, pp. 113–24. In Lee, C. C. (Editor). *Multicultural Issues in Counseling: New Approaches to Diversity* (Third Edition). Alexandria: American Counseling Association.

Solomon, B. B. *The inner-city church: A non-traditional setting for mental health services*, pp. 129–53. In Harvey, A. R. (Editor) (1985). *The Black Family: An Afro-centric Perspective*. New York: United Church of Christ Commission for Racial Justice.

Taylor, R. J., C. G. Ellison, L. M. Chatters, J. S. Levin, and K. D. Lincoln (2000). "Mental Health Services in Faith Communities: The Role of Clergy in Black Churches." *Social Work*. 45, 73–87.

Woodson, C. G. (1921). *The History of the Negro Church*. Washington, D.C.: The Associated Publisher.

CHAPTER 9

Counseling in the Religious Arena—The Potentials and Challenges*

"Study to shew thyself approved unto God, a workman that needeth not to be ashamed, rightly dividing the word of truth."

2 TIMOTHY 2:15

■

"Brethren, if a man be overtaken in a fault, ye which are spiritual, restore such an one in the spirit of meekness; considering thyself, lest thou also be tempted. Bear ye one another's burdens, and so fulfil the law of Christ."

GALATIANS 6:1–2

■

"Confess your faults one to another, and pray one for another, that ye may be healed. The effectual fervent prayer of a righteous man availeth much."

JAMES 5:16

*This chapter is an expansion of a paper originally presented at the National Conference on Biblical Counseling in Philadelphia, PA, on May 18–20, 2000.

INTRODUCTION

The subjects of mental health and psychological counseling were discussed in the preceding chapter. However, there are several reasons why a discussion of counseling in the religious arena is an important topic to address at this time. First, religious-oriented counseling has gained increased attention in the church community as a specific area of focus. Second, there is more emphasis, as noted earlier, on providing counseling and psychological services to parishioners. Third, more pastors, church workers, and congregations are offering counseling and/or allowing counseling services on-site and are favoring a biblical approach. Fourth, seminaries offer programs in pastoral care and counseling and graduates of these programs are likely to set up such programs in the church settings in which they work. Fifth, those congregations that are reluctant to offer general psychological services (though the numbers are increasing) are more open to religious or biblical counseling services.

DEFINITIONS OF COUNSELING

When approaching the topic of counseling, the definition, as well as the area of focus, is a critical matter to consider. Many clients enter counseling having heard various conceptions of the encounter and may be expecting something quite different from what they may experience. This is true of counseling in general as well as within religious settings. Some of the labels that are being used for counseling in the religious realm are:

- Pastoral counseling
- Christian counseling
- Religious counseling
- Spiritual counseling
- Biblical counseling

The similarities and differences in definitions will now be explored.

Pastoral counseling. The American Association of Pastoral Counseling (2001) defines pastoral counseling as:

> a unique form of psychotherapy which uses spiritual resources as well as psychological understanding for healing and growth. It is provided by certified pastoral counselors, who are not only mental health professionals but who have also had in-depth religious and/or theological training.

Wimberly (1989) in a chapter titled "Pastoral Counseling and the Black Perspective" sees pastoral care and counseling in a corporate context. By "corporate," he means that "the care of the individual is a function of the total community rather than the function of the pastor or any other specially designated person who possesses specialized skills" (p. 421). Wimberly (1991) states that the goal of pastoral care and counseling from a narrative perspective "is to use storytelling to strengthen people's personal and interpersonal growth, so that they can respond to God's salvation drama as it unfolds and impacts their lives" (p. 18). He sees pastoral care, an element of pastoral counseling, as "bringing all the resources of the faith story into the context of caring relationships, to bear upon the lives of people as they face life struggles which are personal, interpersonal, and emotional" (p. 18). It has the therapeutic functions of healing, sustaining, guiding, and reconciling. Thus, pastoral counseling occurs under the auspices of a church and is typically done by a member of the ministerial staff.

Christian counseling. Christian counseling is a type of counseling wherein a client is assisted in dealing with issues within the context of his or her Christian faith. Christian counseling is that which is offered by a person trained in the field and who deliberately brings to bear principles of the Christian faith into the counseling process. This may be done by either a member of the ministerial staff or not. Gary Collins (2007) who has written extensively in this area states that "the Christian counselor becomes a spiritual leader who guides spiritual growth, helps counselees deal with spiritual struggles, and enables them to find meaningful beliefs and values" (p. 66).

Religious counseling. Emile Durkheim (1976), a sociologist, defined a religion as "a unified system of beliefs and practices relative to sacred things, that is to say, things set apart and forbidden—beliefs and practices which unite into one single moral community called a Church, all those that adhere to them" (p. 47). Gordon Allport (1950), a psychologist, in the book *The Individual and His Religion* defined an individual's religion as "the audacious bid he makes to bind himself to creation and to the Creator. It is his ultimate attempt to enlarge and to complete his own personality by finding the supreme context in which he rightly belongs" (p. 161).

William James (1958), another psychologist, in his book *The Varieties of Religious Experience* defined religion as: "the feelings, acts, and experiences of individual men in their solitude, so far as they apprehend themselves to stand in relation to whatever they consider the divine" (p. 42). Thus to understand and deal with religion within the religious context, one must attend to the various religious factors included under the definitions.

According to Miller and Thoresen (1999), religious factors involve prescribed beliefs, rituals, and practices, as well as social institutional features. Hence, religious counseling is counseling performed by a trained professional in the context of a religious institution or an institution that is respectful of religious tradition and includes applying principles of any faith tradition. While Christian counseling is one type of religious counseling, religious counseling is a broader concept and focuses on the elements (religious factors) described in the definitions above.

Spiritual counseling. According to Miller and Thoresen (1999), spiritual factors are concerned more with individual subjective experiences. Spirituality is viewed as an attribute of the individual. According to Kurtz (1999), spirituality "denotes 'certain positive inward qualities and perceptions' while avoiding implications of 'narrow, dogmatic beliefs and obligatory religious observances'" (p. 20). Kurtz (1999) further states that:

> The goal of spirituality is the alleviation of mental, emotional, and spiritual distress thought to be at least in part caused by the lack of an appropriate relationship with ultimate reality,

most often signaled by and reflected in inappropriate relationships with other people and things. Spirituality is less a method than an attitude . . . (p. 20).

Cashwell and Young (2005) discussed the complexities as well as the difficulties in defining the term "spiritual." Spiritual counseling, therefore, is counseling that aids in helping a person to deal with inner subjective experiences and their conception of the "divine" and "ultimate reality." Such counseling is thus very broad and is typically disconnected with a specific faith tradition or religious institution.

Biblical counseling. Biblical counseling seeks to assist an individual in solving his or her problems using the Bible as the source of authority. Clarence Walker in his book *Biblical Counseling with African-Americans* (1992) defined biblical counseling as "that which is based on a sound biblical foundation; incorporates both Christian and secular theory where consistent with scripture; and is relevant to the unique ethnic characteristics peculiar to Black people" (p. 9). Lawrence Crabb in his book *Basic Principles of Biblical Counseling* (1975) describes a biblical approach to counseling as that "which asserts the authority of Scripture and the necessity and adequacy of Christ" (p. 15). By "biblical counseling," I mean the application of the relevancy and authority of Scriptures in a counseling relationship where the aim or goal is to bring about change in the life of the person being counseled by using specific scriptures or biblically related techniques or principles.

The Association of Biblical Counseling (2005) defines biblical counseling as:

any gentle instruction, encouragement, or rebuke of one brother or sister in Christ. It happens both informally (i.e., while standing around after church), as well as formally (i.e., in a pastor's office). It reflects and is based on sound biblical teaching and a dependence on a risen Lord.

BROADER DEFINITIONAL ISSUES—
SPIRITUAL AND SPIRITUALITY

To further illustrate the complication of definitions, consider the statement by Hogue in the chapter "Religion in America: The Demographics of Belief and Affiliation" in the book edited by Edward Shafranske entitled *Religion and the Clinical Practice of Psychology* (1996). Hogue states:

> The topic is laden with definitional problems. Not only are sociologists inconsistent in their concepts and definitions, but the varied and imprecise use of terms by the mass media makes matters worse, as well. Good examples are the varied meanings of the words *cult* and *spirituality*. Some Americans today describe themselves as "spiritual but not religious," and this usually means that their spiritual beliefs and behaviors are not associated with any traditional church or synagogue . . . To compound the problem, the term *spiritual* has such vague and unbounded meanings that it is barely useful, and it fits poorly —if at all—with prevailing psychological theories. One's only option, in the face of this confusion, is to set forth the necessary definitions and distinctions at the beginning of any exposition. I will distinguish five entities: religious preference, church affiliation, church involvement, religious belief, and personal religious behavior (pp. 21–22).

Hogue gives the following definitions of the above five entities (p. 22):

- Religious preference—is a person's feeling of whether he or she belongs to a religious group.
- Church affiliation—is a measure of whether a person belongs to a church or synagogue in the sense of having his or her name on a membership list.
- Church involvement—is mainly a matter of church attendance, but it also includes participation in groups or committees in the church, financial contributions to the church, and socialization with other parishioners.
- Religious belief—includes belief in God and divine teachings as found in sacred writings.
- Personal religious behavior—includes prayer; devotional readings; study of religious texts; meditation; and other behaviors, such as keeping dietary rules, that are seen as spiritually beneficial. It is distinct from church-going or ongoing participation groups.

All of these factors must be assessed and taken into consideration when working with a person around religious concerns.

Spirituality or spiritual, as a concept, apart from organized religion or Christianity, is becoming more of a force to be reckoned with. Increasingly, as already noted, more people are comfortable in declaring themselves as spiritual, but without having a specific religious affiliation.

However, in a biblical context, the word "spiritual" as used in the New Testament is defined by Scofield (1998) as "non-carnal." Speaking to this concept in 1 Corinthians 2:12–16, the apostle Paul states:

Now we have received, not the spirit of the world, but the spirit which is of God; that we might know the things that are freely given to us of God. Which things also we speak, not in the words which man's wisdom teacheth, but which the Holy

Ghost teacheth; comparing spiritual things with spiritual. But the natural man receiveth not the things of the Spirit of God: for they are foolishness unto him: neither can he know them, because they are spiritually discerned. But he that is spiritual judgeth all things, yet he himself is judged of no man. For who hath known the mind of the LORD, that he may instruct him? But we have the mind of Christ.

While the Bible makes reference to "spiritual wickedness in high places" (Ephesians 6:12), spirituality in the Christian context is very precise. It is the result of a connection to God as defined in the Bible and is produced by reliance on the Holy Spirit. Vine (1981) in discussing the word "spiritual" indicates that the spiritual person is one who walks by the Spirit (Holy Spirit) and manifests His fruit. With the blurring and confusion of terms, biblical counselors must clearly assess where a client is on the various dimensions of religion, including a clear assessment of what is meant by "spiritual" and "spirituality."

RELUCTANCE AND THE COUNSELING PROCESS

Research has shown that people of color, in general, utilize counseling and therapeutic services differently from Whites (refer to June, 1986; Leong, Wagner, and Tata, 1995). For example, people of color tend to:

- use counseling services at a fairly low rate
- exhibit reluctance to engage in the counseling process
- drop out of counseling at a high rate
- often prefer a counselor of the same race
- be frequently misdiagnosed
- be seen in therapy for short periods of time
- have short hospital stays

- have more contact with paraprofessional staff than do Whites
- experience comparatively more stress than do Whites
- be often disadvantaged by traditional psychological assessments
- seek help for administrative matters (i.e., problems with the law, social services agencies, and schools), medication, and questions about help sources in the community rather than personal problems
- use informal help sources in the community (for example, the church).

It is also known from research that men and women often approach helping resources differently. For Black men, the research suggests that they (see June, 1986):

- are not high disclosers
- seek treatment most often for depression or work-related problems
- experience high levels of stress and are at high risk for suicidal and homicidal behaviors

What the Profession of Psychology and Counseling Is Now Teaching in Regard to Religion

Over the last few decades, the general field of psychology and the area of mental health have become more accepting of religion and faith issues. Furthermore, religion is considered an important aspect of mental health and proper mental health functioning. For the biblical counselor—this is both good and bad news. It is good news in the sense that if a Christian now goes to a nonreligious or secular counselor, he or she is more likely to be more accepted or respected for his/her religious beliefs and will be engaged in the therapeutic encounter around his or her religious concerns. However, this greater acceptance may be bad news in the sense that the nonreligious or secular counselor will probably only be able to deal with the concern in a global sense or according to his or her definition and understanding of the term "spiritual." Potentially damaging will be those instances wherein the issue of concern is one that involves clear scriptural mandates or positions that may be at odds with general societal or psychological views.

Professional codes of ethics in general counseling and psychology have evolved to the point where they specifically mention the area of religion. For example, in the current *American Counseling Association Code of Ethics* (2005), the following is stated under Section C, Professional Responsibility:

> C.5. Nondiscrimination. Counselors do not condone or engage in discrimination based on age, culture, disability, ethnicity, race, *religion/spirituality*, gender, gender identity, sexual orientation, marital status/partnership, language preference, socioeconomic status, or any basis proscribed by law (italics mine).

In the current *Ethical Principles of Psychologists and Code of Conduct* (2002), which became effective June 1, 2003, the following is stated under General Principles:

> Principle E: Respect for People's Rights and Dignity. Psychologists are aware of and respect cultural, individual, and role differences, including those based on age, gender identity, race, ethnicity, culture, national origin, *religion*, sexual orientation, disability, language, and socioeconomic status and consider these factors when working with members of such groups. Psychologists try to eliminate the effect on their work of biases based on those factors, and they do not knowingly participate

in or condone activities of others based upon such prejudices (italics mine).

Under the Ethical Standards, in regard to competence, the following is stated:

2.01 Boundaries of Competence. (a) Psychologists provide services, teach, and conduct research with populations and in areas only within the boundaries of their competence, based on their education, training, supervised experience, consultation, study, or professional experience.

In the book *A Spiritual Strategy for Counseling and Psychotherapy* (1997, p. 120), Richards and Bergin offer eleven characteristics of what they call effective ecumenical therapists. According to them, effective ecumenical therapists:

- are aware of their own religious and spiritual heritage, worldview assumptions, and values and are sensitive to how their own spiritual issues, values, and biases could affect their work with clients from different religious and spiritual traditions.
- seek to understand, respect, and appreciate religious and spiritual traditions, worldviews, and values that are different from their own.
- are capable of communicating interest, understanding, and respect to clients who have religious and spiritual worldviews, beliefs, and values that are different from the therapist.
- seek to understand how a client's religious and spiritual worldview and values affect the client's sense of identity, lifestyle, and emotional and interpersonal functioning, but they are also sensitive to how their own religious

175

and spiritual values and beliefs could bias their
judgment.
- are sensitive to circumstances (e.g., personal biases, value
  conflicts, lack of knowledge of the client's religious tradition) that could dictate referral of a religious client to
  a member of his or her religious tradition.
- have or seek specific knowledge and information about
  the religious beliefs and traditions of the religious and
  spiritual clients with whom they work.
- avoid making assumptions about the beliefs and values
  of religious and spiritual clients based on religious affiliation alone, but they seek to gain an in-depth understanding of each client's unique spiritual worldview,
  beliefs, and values.
- understand how to sensitively handle value and belief
  conflicts that arise during therapy and do so in a manner that preserves the client's autonomy and self-esteem.
- make efforts to establish respectful, trusting relationships with members and leaders in their clients' religious community and seek to draw on these sources of
  social support to benefit their clients when appropriate.
- seek to understand the religious and spiritual resources
  in their clients' lives and encourage their clients to use
  these resources to assist them in their efforts to cope,
  heal, and change.
- seek to use religious and spiritual interventions that are
  in harmony with their clients' religious and spiritual beliefs when it appears that such interventions could help
  their client cope, heal, and change.

The use of the designation "ecumenical therapists" raises interesting questions for both the profession of psychology and for
the field of biblical counseling. For instance, "Can one really be

such a person and if so how effective can one be across the wide spectrum of religious beliefs and traditions?"

In the book *Integrating Spirituality and Religion into Counseling: A Guide to Competent Practice*, Cashwell and Young (2005a) list nine competencies that they believe are essential for a therapist to possess in order to be considered spiritually competent. According to them, the professional counselor:

- can explain the relationship between religion and spirituality, including similarities and differences.
- can describe religious and spiritual beliefs and practices in a cultural context.
- engages in self-exploration of religious and spiritual beliefs in order to increase sensitivity, understanding, and acceptance of diverse belief systems.
- can describe her or his religious and/or spiritual belief system and explain various models of religious or spiritual development across the life span.
- can demonstrate sensitivity and acceptance of a variety of religious and/or spiritual expressions in client communication.
- can identify limits of his or her understanding of a client's religious or spiritual expression and demonstrate appropriate referral skills and generate possible referral sources.
- can assess the relevance of the religious and/or spiritual domains in the client's therapeutic issues.
- is sensitive to and receptive of religious and/or spiritual themes in the counseling process as befits the expressed preference of each client.
- uses a client's religious and/or spiritual beliefs in the pursuit of the client's therapeutic goals as befits the client's expressed preference.

These expected competencies, like those for the ecumenical therapist, are on paper very admirable but the real question is whether a therapist or counselor in general can possess all of these characteristics.

DECIDING ON AN APPROACH OR APPROACHES—
REFLECTIONS ON BIBLICAL COUNSELING

This and the next few sections will focus on the specific area of biblical counseling. Biblical counseling is no different from general counseling on this dimension. Within the field of general counseling, there are numerous approaches to counseling and theories of counseling. In the area of biblical or biblically related counseling, while the number of approaches is not as numerous as in general counseling, one can also be trained in different approaches. For example, one can draw and use the approaches and techniques of the following (just to name a few):

- Jay Adams (1970)
- Lawrence Crabb Jr. (1975; 1977)
- Gary Collins (2007)
- Clyde Narramore (1960)
- Clarence Walker (1992)
- Edward Wimberly (1989; 1991)
- Everett Worthington Jr. (1999)

THE OPPORTUNITIES FOR BIBLICAL COUNSELING

Biblical counseling is needed for several reasons. First of all, the Bible in a broad sense supports it. Secondly, society itself is undergoing unprecedented change in all areas and the church is not excluded. A new "change" vocabulary has been advanced as demonstrated by the following words:

- benchmarks
- best practices
- branding
- breaking down silos
- collaboration
- continuous quality improvement (CQI)
- cross-training
- customers
- customer-driven
- cyberspace
- demographer
- distance learning
- do more with less
- downsizing
- economies
- effectiveness
- efficiency
- entrenchment
- focus groups
- global village
- information highways
- information technologies
- in-forming
- insourcing
- managed care
- market-driven
- market share
- mission statement
- offshoring
- open-sourcing
- outsourcing
- outcomes
- paperless
- paradigm shift
- performance indicators
- privatization
- re-engineering
- seamless
- strategic planning
- supply-chaining
- target specific
- thinking out of the box
- total quality management
- transformation
- virtual reality
- virtual universities
- visioning

Books such as *The World is Flat* (Friedman, 2005) are helpful in regard to learning the general change vocabulary. One could also develop a similar list of new concepts/terminologies that have entered the Christian community and that list would include many words from the above list.

In a book entitled *Church Next—Quantum Changes in How We Do Ministry* (2000), Gibbs shares several changes that

are taking place which Christians, church leaders, and counselors need to be aware of and consider. These include changes
from:

- living in the past to engaging with the present
- market-driven to mission-oriented
- bureaucratic hierarchies to apostolic networks
- schooling professionals to mentoring leaders
- following celebrities to encountering saints
- dead orthodoxy to living faith
- attracting a crowd to seeking the lost
- belonging to believing
- generic congregations to incarnational communities

Gibbs (2000) suggests that the world we live in has moved
from what philosophers and sociologists call modernity to postmodernity. He defines modernity as:

an understanding of the world through an autonomous and
human rationality. Evangelicalism arose within that context,
which meant that it had to confront the challenges of human-
ism and rationalism. In so doing it was itself influenced, much
more than it realized, by the modernism it combated (p. 22).

Modernity, according to Gibbs (2000), has pushed the overall church to leave little place for revelation or the "mysteries
of God" and to encourage:

the separation of lives into public and private sphere and its
compartmentalization into specialized areas resulted in religious faith becoming marginalized from society and reduced to
a privatized matter for likeminded individuals to pursue without imposing their views on the public sphere (p. 22).

This almost complete separation of lives into public and private spheres is probably one of the major problems for Christians resulting in Christianity being not viewed as a lifestyle.

Postmodernity, according to Gibbs, is characterized by:

- a world where technical knowledge has advanced beyond our wisdom
- pessimism and skepticism
- truth that is redefined in terms of consensus and "whatever works for you"
- the rejection of prepositional certainty
- the celebration of diversity
- no place for God
- the church as marginalized

CHARACTERISTICS THAT
BIBLICAL COUNSELORS MUST POSSESS

Attempts have been made to describe the characteristics that must be possessed by the ecumenical and the professional counselor who is skilled in integrating spirituality and religion into counseling. What, then, must be the characteristics and competencies of biblical counselors who operate in this postmodern world?

I would offer that biblical counselors must be:

- well versed in the Scriptures and able to properly interpret them. The Bible exhorts believers to "Study to shew thyself approved unto God, a workman that needeth not to be ashamed, rightly dividing the word of truth" (2 Timothy 2:15).
- well trained in the field of biblical counseling but with supplemental skills in the area of general counseling.

- keenly aware of the influences of society and how these can influence and affect Christians and churches.
- aware of the teachings of the "multiple religious teachers," many of which distort the Bible.
- aware of how the "multiple teachers" are influencing church members and clients and thus often creating problems for those served.
- conscious of how biblical Christianity is being redefined.
- aware of the electronic church and electronic "pastors/preachers" and their teachings.
- able to understand and detect toxic faith and erroneous religious beliefs systems.
- culturally sensitive and culturally competent.
- aware of Afrocentricity and its importance.
- dependent on the power and leading of the Holy Spirit.

RESEARCH ON THE BENEFITS OF RELIGION AND CHRISTIANITY TO HEALTH AND WELL-BEING

While an extensive body of research data on the effectiveness of biblical counseling does not exist, there has been research on the benefits of religion in general. Biblical counseling, however, needs to be subjected to rigorous research. Some of the research on the benefits of religion follows. (See Scott Richards and Allen E. Bergin, "Toward Religious and Spiritual Competency for Mental Health Professionals" in the *Handbook of Psychotherapy and Religious Diversity* [2000, p. 14.])

- Religiously committed people tend to report greater subjective well-being and life satisfaction.
- People who engage in religious coping (e.g., praying, reading sacred writings, meditating, seeking support

from religious leaders and community) during stressful times tend to adjust better to crises and problems.

- Intrinsic (devout) religious people tend to experience less anxiety, including less death anxiety. They also tend to be more free of worry and neurotic guilt.
- Religious commitment is usually associated with less depression. Among elderly people, church attendance is strongly predictive of less depression.
- People who attend church are less likely to divorce. Studies have also consistently shown a positive relationship between religious participation and marital satisfaction and adjustment.
- People with high levels of religious involvement are less likely to use or abuse alcohol. There is also extensive evidence that religiously committed people are less likely to use or abuse drugs.
- Religious denominations that have clear, unambiguous prohibitions against premarital sex have lower rates of premarital sex and teenage pregnancy.
- Religious commitment, as measured by church attendance, is associated negatively with delinquency.
- Religiously committed people report fewer suicidal impulses, report more negative attitudes toward suicide, and commit suicide less often than nonreligious people.
- Religious commitment is associated positively with moral behavior. Devoutly religious people generally adhere to more stringent moral standards, curbing personal desire or gain to promote the welfare of others and of society (e.g., not gambling, drinking, or engaging in premarital or extramarital sex).
- Intrinsic religious commitment is associated positively with empathy and altruism.

- Religious commitment is associated positively with better physical health. Religious people have a lower prevalence of a wide range of illnesses, including cancer, cardiovascular disease, and hypertension.
- As a group, religiously committed people tend to live longer and to respond better once they have been diagnosed with an illness.
- People's religious beliefs can help them cope better with their illnesses, including a reduced likelihood of severe depression and perceived disability.
- Religiously committed surgical patients have shown lower rates of postoperative mortality, less depression, and better ambulation status than patients with lower levels of religious commitment.

Wallace and Forman (1998) also showed some of the benefits of religion for American youth. Drawing from a large sample taken from the University of Michigan's Monitoring the Future Project, approximately 5,000 youth were studied. They found that compared to their peers, religious youth (those who saw religion as important and were regular attendees) were less likely to engage in behaviors that compromise their health. For example: behaviors such as carrying weapons, getting into fights, and drinking and driving were cited. Additionally, religious youth were more likely to behave in ways that enhance their health. For example, proper nutrition, exercise, and rest.

Chatters (2000) and Taylor, Chatters, and Levin (2004) may also be consulted for a summary of some of the research on religion and health generally and in reference to Black Americans.

BIBLICAL COUNSELING—
OPPORTUNITIES FOR MULTIPLE INTERVENTIONS

One of the major contributions of community psychology to the counseling field is the conceptualization of various approaches to prevention and intervention. These are:

- Primary prevention/systems intervention (see for example, Rappaport, 1977; and Dalton, Elias and Wandersman, 2001). This approach rests on the belief that problems or issues are often the result of the way systems operate, policies are implemented, structures are put in place, etc. The assumption is that in order to eliminate or treat the problem one must make an intervention at the systems level; that is, at the level of institutions, policies, and structures. This is the approach that Dr. Willie Richardson basically takes in the book *Reclaiming the Urban Family—How to Mobilize the Church as a Family Training Center* (1996).
- Secondary prevention/group intervention. This approach rests on the belief that problems or issues are the result of the way groups operate. The assumption is that in order to eliminate or treat the problem one must make changes or interventions at the group level.
- Tertiary prevention/individual intervention. This approach rests on the belief that problems or issues are the result of deficiencies in the individual. The assumption is that in order to eliminate or treat the problem one must make an intervention at the individual level.

Such a conceptualization is consistent with Wimberly's view of pastoral counseling and care as corporate. Why are these concepts important to the biblical counselors and the church in its approach to biblical counseling? An understanding and implementation of these approaches are necessary for at least the following reasons:

- Not all problems/issues need individual or small group counseling.
- No matter how skilled individual counselors are, many persons will not seek out counseling.
- Individual and small group counseling are time consuming and if they are the only options they are inefficient, at least for certain issues.
- Therapeutic communities need to be built. Communities cannot be built effectively by just dealing with individuals. The church is a community—the Body of Christ.
- Applying individual interventions to problems that stem from group and system-level issues will result in what William Ryan (1971) calls "blaming the victim."

RELATIONSHIPS WITH BLACK MENTAL HEALTH PROFESSIONALS WHO ARE CHRISTIANS

While there are few national associations of predominantly Black Christian counselors, social workers, counselors, or therapists (The Association of Biblical Counselors is the exception), there is a Division of the American Association of Christian Counselors Association. This division is called the Black African-American Christian Counselors (www.AACC.net).

There are increasing numbers of Black Christian counselors, psychologists, social workers, psychologists, and psychiatrists throughout the nation. Biblical counseling professionals must network with such professionals. This responsibility is true for both sides.

CONCLUSION

The possibilities for positive working relationships between the field of psychology and the church community clearly exist. However, there are numerous challenges that must be faced head-on by both communities. In this chapter, the basic tension points have been addressed and suggestions have been made to help resolve them.

REFERENCES

Adams, J. E. (1970). *Competent to Counsel.* Grand Rapids: Baker Books.

Allport, G. W. (1950). *The Individual and His Religion.* New York: MacMillan.

American Association of Pastoral Counseling (2001). Defining "Pastoral Counseling." www.counselingcenter.org/pastoral. htm

American Counseling Association Code of Ethics (2005). Annapolis: American Counseling Association. www.counseling. org/ethics

American Psychological Association Ethical Principles of Psychologists and Code of Conduct (December 2002). *American Psychologist.* 57, 1060–73.

Association of Biblical Counseling (2005). What is Biblical Counseling? www.christiancounseling.com

Cashwell, C. S. and J. S. Young (Editors) (2005a). *Integrating Spirituality and Religion into Counseling: A Guide to Competent Practice.* Alexandria: American Counseling Association.

Cashwell, C. S. and J. S. Young (2005b). *Integrating Spirituality and Religion Into Counseling: An Introduction,* pp. 1–9. In Cashwell, C. S. and J. S. Young (Editors). *Integrating Spirituality and Religion into Counseling: A Guide to Competent Practice.* Alexandria: American Counseling Association.

Chatters, L. M. (2000). "Religion and Health: Public Health Research and Practice." *Annual Review of Public Health.* 21, 335–67.

Collins, G. (2007). *Christian Counseling: A Comprehensive Guide* (Third Edition). Dallas: Thomas Nelson.

Crabb, L. Jr. (1975). *Basic Principles of Biblical Counseling.* Grand Rapids: Zondervan.

_____ (1977). *Effective Biblical Counseling: A Model for Helping Caring Christians Become Capable Counselors.* Grand Rapids: Zondervan.

Dalton, J. H., M. J. Elias, and A. Wandersman (2001). *Community Psychology: Linking Individuals and Communities.* Belmont: Wadsworth.

Durkheim, E. (1976). *The Elementary Forms of the Religious Life* (Second Edition). London: George Allen and Unwin LTD.

Friedman, T. L. (2005). *The World is Flat: A Brief History of the Twenty-First Century.* New York: Farrar, Straus, and Giroux.

Gibbs, E. (2000). *Church Next: Quantum Changes in How We Do Ministry.* Downers Grove: InterVarsity Press.

Hogue, D. R. (1996). *Religion in America: The Demographics of Belief and Affiliation.* In Shafranske, E. P. (1996). *Religion and the Clinical Practice of Psychology.* Washington, D.C.: American Psychological Association.

James, W. (1958). *The Varieties of Religious Experience.* New York: Signet.

June, L. N. (1986). "Enhancing the Delivery of Mental Health and Counseling Services to Black Males: Critical Agency and Provider Responsibilities," *Journal of Multicultural Counseling and Development,* 14, 39–45.

Kurtz, E. (1999). *The Historical Context.* In Miller, W. R.

(Editor), *Integrating Spirituality into Treatment: Resources for Practitioners*. Washington, D.C.: American Psychological Association, 19–46.

Leong, F. T. L., N. S. Wagner, and S. P. Tata (1995). *Racial and Ethnic Variations in Help-Seeking Attitudes*. In Ponterotto, J. G., J. M. Casas, L. A. Suzuki, and C. M. Alexander (Editors), *Handbook of Multicultural Counseling*. Thousand Oaks: Sage Publications.

Miller, W. R. and C. E. Thoresen (1999). *Spirituality and Health*. In Miller, W. R. (Editor), *Integrating Spirituality into Treatment: Resources for Practitioners*. Washington, D.C.: American Psychological Association, 3–18.

Miller, W. R. (Editor) (1999). *Integrating Spirituality into Treatment: Resources for Practitioners*. Washington, D.C.: American Psychological Association.

Narramore, C. M. (1960). *The Psychology of Counseling*. Grand Rapids: Zondervan.

Rappaport, J. (1977). *Community Psychology: Values, Research, and Action*. Chicago: Holt, Reinhart and Winston.

Richards, P. S. and A. E. Bergin (2000). *Toward Religious and Spiritual Competency for Mental Health Professionals*. In Richards, P. S. and A. E. Bergin (Editors) (2000). *Handbook of Psychotherapy and Religious Diversity*. Washington, D.C.: American Psychological Association.

_____ (1997). *A Spiritual Strategy for Counseling and Psychotherapy*. Washington, D.C.: American Psychological Association.

Richards, P. S. and A. E. Bergin (Editors) (2000). *Handbook of Psychotherapy and Religious Diversity*. Washington, D.C.: American Psychological Association.

Richardson, W. (1996). *Reclaiming the Urban Family: How to Mobilize the Church as a Family Training Center.* Grand Rapids: Zondervan.

Ryan, W. (1971). *Blaming the Victim.* New York: Vintage Books.

Scofield, C. I. (Editor) (1998). *The New Scofield Study Bible: Authorized King James Version.* New York: Oxford.

Shafranske, E. P. (1996). *Religion and the Clinical Practice of Psychology.* Washington, D.C.: American Psychological Association.

Strong, J. (1996). *The New Strong's Exhaustive Concordance of the Bible.* Nashville: Thomas Nelson.

Taylor, R. J., L. M. Chatters, and J. Levin (2004). *Religion in the Lives of African Americans—Social, Psychological, and Health Perspectives.* Thousands Oaks: Sage Publications.

Vine, W. E. (1981). *Vine's Expository Dictionary of Old and New Testament Words.* Old Tappan: Fleming H. Revell.

Walker, C. (1992). *Biblical Counseling with African-Americans: Taking a Ride in the Ethiopian's Chariot.* Grand Rapids: Zondervan.

Wallace, J. M. and T. A. Forman (1998). "Religion's Role in Promoting Health and Reducing Risk Among American Youth." *Health Education and Behavior.* 25, 721–41.

Wimberly, E. P. (1989). Pastoral Care and the Black Perspective. In Wilmore, G. S. (Editor). *African American Religious Studies: An Interdisciplinary Anthology.* Durham: Duke University Press.

_____ (1991). *African American Pastoral Care.* Nashville: Abingdon Press.

Worthington, E. L. Jr. (1999). *Hope-Focused Marriage Counseling: A Guide to Brief Therapy.* Downers Grove: Inter-Varsity Press.

PART FIVE

THE CHURCH—
LIVING UP TO ITS
FULL POTENTIAL

Maximizing the
Church's Full Potential

▪

From Beautiful Buildings
to a Beautiful Church

▪

Resources to Assist in Realizing
the Church's Full Potential

CHAPTER 10

Maximizing the Church's Full Potential

"Ye are the salt of the earth: but if the salt have lost
his savour, wherewith shall it be salted? it is
thenceforth good for nothing, but to be cast out, and
to be trodden under foot of men."

MATTHEW 5:13

"Let your light so shine before men,
that they may see your good works,
and glorify your Father which is in heaven."

MATTHEW 5:16

"By this shall all men know that ye are my disciples,
if ye have love one to another."

JOHN 13:35

INTRODUCTION

This chapter will focus on the enduring influence and continued tremendous potential of the church community and ways in which this community can better realize its potential.

Lincoln and Mamiya (1990) estimated that 86% of Black Americans were Christians (80% were in seven major denominations and another 6 percent were in the smaller communions). Further, according to them, the following were characteristic of African Americans and/or "African-American churches" in the 1980s:

- Approximately 78% of all African Americans claimed church membership and attended church services at least once in a six-month period.
- African Americans had slightly higher weekly attendance rates (40%).
- African Americans had the highest rate of being what the sociologists call "super churched" (attending more than once weekly (37% versus 31%).
- African American denominations had not experienced severe declines in membership experienced by some mainstream White denominations like the Disciples of Christ (40%), the United Presbyterian Church (33%), or the Episcopal Church (33%).

Gallup and Jones (2000) found in their survey that 96% of all American adults believed in God or a universal spirit. For Blacks, Gallup and Jones reported that virtually 100% indicated a belief in God or a higher power. Thus given these percentages, the Protestant Christian church community has a large impact on individuals in America and particularly the Black and White populations.

UPDATING THE STATISTICS

Updating Lincoln and Mamiya's church membership data (they estimated a total membership of 23,700,000 in the 1980s) and using the same percentages they used, it would be estimated that of the African American population (36,023,000 of the total 282,082,000 as of March 2002; see Current Population Statistics for constant updates), that 28,097,940 of the 36,023,000 (78%) are church members and have attended services at least once in the last six months. The remaining 7,925,060 or 22% of the 36,023,000 African Americans are not church members and have not attended a service in a six-month period.

If the estimate of the number of African American Christian congregations is correct (75,000), then there is theoretically one congregation for every 480 African Americans (in making this statement, I am well aware that many African Americans are members of predominantly White congregations).

Barna's data (2004a) regarding African Americans reveal the following:

- 57% of African Americans compared to 39% of adults nationwide were more likely to say they were a "born-again Christian" (2001 data).
- 21% were unchurched compared to 39% of Whites (1998 data).

- 53% attended church services on a given Sunday (2002 data).
- The typical "Black church" had an average attendance that was about 50% greater than that of the typical "White church" (1997 data).

In a report of a nationwide survey of more than 2600 adults, titled "Ethnic Groups Differ Substantially on Matters of Faith (Barna, 2004b), the finding was that Blacks were the segment with the most traditional Christian beliefs and practices. Specifically, Barna found that Blacks had the highest percentage on the following dimensions compared to Whites, Asians, and Hispanics:

- read the Bible in the last week
- attended religious service in the past week
- prayed to God in the last week
- participated in a small group in the past week
- strongly agreed that the Bible is totally accurate
- strongly disagreed that Jesus Christ sinned while on earth
- was a born-again Christian

Additionally, Blacks had the lowest percentage that said they were atheist or agnostic (see Table 4 on the following page).

Table 4
RELIGIOUS BELIEFS AND PRACTICES, BY RACE
(Source: The Barna Group, Ventura, CA, 2004)

	White	Black	Hispanic	Asian
Read the Bible in the last week	36%	59%	39%	20%
Attended religious service in the past week	41%	48%	38%	23%
Prayed to God in the past week	81%	91%	86%	46%
Participated in a small group, past week	16%	31%	27%	13%
Bible is totally accurate (strongly agree)	36%	57%	40%	24%
Satan is not a living being (strongly disagree)	30%	27%	30%	14%
Jesus Christ sinned while on earth (strongly disagree)	37%	49%	35%	22%
Born-again Christian	41%	47%	29%	12%
Atheist or agnostic	12%	5%	7%	20%
Align with a non-Christian faith	11%	12%	10%	45%
Subgroup size	**1695**	**330**	**360**	**94**

These data show the continual critical role and the influence of the "Black Church" in the lives of African Americans.

SOME QUESTIONS RAISED BY THE STATISTICS

Given these statistics, the "Black Church" continues to be in touch with most of the Black population (though there is an increasing number of African Americans who are attending and/or members of a predominantly White congregation— a phenomenon that needs studying). With this large reach, questions must be raised, such as, why is there not a greater impact on certain negative behaviors within the African American community? Why are there more men between certain ages in prison than in college? Why are the HIV AIDS infection rates so high? Why in certain ways does there appear to be an over-all "moral decline"?

One response to this set of questions could be that it is un-fair to place these issues at the feet of the church. Another an-swer might be that these are complicated issues and it takes more than the church to solve them. Another answer might be that congregations vary tremendously in terms of impact based on their typology or model. However, whatever the answer might be, one should pause to ask the further question of whether the church is realizing its full potential. Can and could the church be doing more? If indeed the church and Christians are "the salt of the earth" and "the light of the world," then something must be wrong. In addition, what is the major reli-gious challenge to Christianity?

According to Keller (2000), "The largest religious group in the world is Christianity with a total world membership of approximately 1,929,987,000 or 33% of the world popula-tion" (p. 28). Hence, approximately two billion of the world's population of six billion at this point in time were Christians.

Islam is the second largest religion in the world with a mem-bership of 1,147,494,000 or 19.6% of the world's population. Keller (2000) stated that 300 million of these are in Africa and 4.06 million are in North America. However, other estimates of the number of Muslims in North America are higher.

In reference to Islam, Lincoln and Mamiya (1990) have noted that it has become particularly attractive to young Black males in America. They quoted a *New York Times* article, which es-timated that in 1989 approximately one million of the six mil-lion Muslims in America were Black and made the following observation:

A full decade before the turn of the twenty-first century, if the estimate of 6 million Muslims in the United States is reasonably accurate, Islam has become the second largest religion in America, after Protestant and Catholic Christianity. American Judaism with a steadily declining membership is now third. While much more of this Islamic growth is independent of the black community, the possibility of serious impact on the Black Church cannot be peremptorily dismissed. The phenomenon of more black males preferring Islam while more black females adhere to traditional black Christianity is not as bizarre as it sounds. It is already clear that in Islam the historic black church denominations will be faced with a far more serious and more powerful competitor for the souls of black folk than the white churches ever were. When is the question, not whether (p. 391).

Why is Islam very attractive to African American males and what must be done to make Christianity more attractive? In reference to this question, Lincoln and Mamiya (1990) suggested that the symbols of manhood projected by such prominent Muslims as Malcolm X and Muhammad Ali are factors. While this is undoubtedly true, Islam is also more aggressive in its outreach to males, particularly in the prison environment.

THREE PITFALLS TO AVOID

Pitfall One: The Functional Autonomy of Christianity. In observing what is occurring in some circles today, could one say that many churchgoers are searching for a "religious" experience devoid of the historical biblical expectation and expected commitment to Christ? That is, it seems that for some there is an awareness of the deep and rich faith heritage of our fore-parents, a concomitant desire to continue that heritage, but without replicating the historically deep commitment.

Where this happens, one finds only the symbols of Christianity, the trappings of Christianity, the aura of Christianity, the sounds of Christianity, the dress of Christianity, the words of Christianity, the beat of Christianity, and the "entertainment" of Christianity. One thus finds as an old TV commercial once highlighted "Parkay, but no butter." I will describe the phenomenon as the functional autonomy of Christianity. Where this happens, the result is that the maximum benefits of Christianity have moved *outside* of the "Black Church." When this happens, church attendance and membership may still be high, offerings may be higher, and the songs at first glance may sound the same, but upon closer scrutiny they are devoid of the deeper meanings and feelings. The pastor may still say the same things, but the words may produce different results. When this happens, the church has lost some of its grip on the people—or the salt still looks like salt but has lost its savor. When this happens, the church has lost its ability to be the healing community.

Many Christians and congregations do not fit the above descriptions. Such are still deeply committed, authentic, and providing the benefits of a healing community. Jesus Christ and the full spiritual and psychological benefits for them are still in the church. But even for those who are authentic and committed, it becomes increasingly difficult to reap and enjoy the full benefits of the healing community within this overall new environment.

Pitfall Two: Serving Two Masters. Jesus said, "No one can serve two masters. Either he will hate the one and love the other, or he will be devoted to the one and despise the other. You cannot serve both God and Money" (Matthew 6:24 NIV). James said, "Pure religion and undefiled before God and the Father is this, To visit the fatherless and widows in their affliction, and to keep himself unspotted from the world" (James 1:27).

Seemingly, some Christians are trying to serve two masters. With the rich religious heritage that Blacks have; with the desire to maintain some semblance of that heritage; with increased opportunities for self-expressions, particularly for the more formally educated and trained; and with Christianity becoming less taught, expected, and practiced as a way of life—the Black Christian is increasingly experiencing split loyalties. Jobs, occupations, and careers are not seen or taught as ministries but simply as ways of making money. Under such a scenario, attending church services can thus become merely weekly rituals and ways to satisfy a religious conscience.

The church community, under such circumstances, becomes a necessary link to a historical past but a modern-day pacifier or in some cases a mere "entertainment center." This phenomenon is something that Dr. Martin Luther King Jr. warned against in the sermon "Guidelines for a Constructive Church" (Carson and Holloron, 1998). Though the church is still the most powerful institution in our community as the statistics and other data suggest, it is losing some of its grip and, in many instances, is more irrelevant to the "deeper" lives of the people than was the case in the past. For many, it has become the "sear" of an authentic religious conscious. For others, it is a way to appease a religious conscience.

We see this serving of two masters when one experiences no conflict with two obviously contradictory lifestyles. Such persons can earn money in a profession that would have historically been called sin and at the same time be highly praised in the church community. Such persons can engage in questionable activities and feel no real sense of remorse and are even open about this in the "Christian" community. Persons, for example, who win the lottery, even within some church communities will often boldly proclaim that it is a "blessing" from God.

We see this serving of two masters when recent converts who are celebrities become instant religious experts. One has to wonder along with Karl Menninger (1973) and also ask the question: "What ever became of sin?"

Pitfall Three: Ministers without Ministries. Another pitfall to avoid is becoming a "minister without a ministry." How can that be, you ask? I would suggest that it could happen because of organizational or individual factors.

On the organizational side, there are "ministers" without ministry when the church structure is such that the spiritual gifts of individuals are not identified and are not allowed to operate. As indicated in a prior chapter, my belief is that all Christians are ministers in a biblical sense and thus have a role to carry out in the corporate body. However, because of a misunderstanding of certain Scriptures, a narrow definition of ministry, misguided views of authority, personal insecurities and/or perceived threats, spiritual gifts are not allowed to be exercised and the individual with a particular gift is frustrated and not allowed to do what would help the Body of Christ to grow. In other instances, the organizational problems or structure may be such that the individual's spiritual gift is recognized and the individual attempts to exercise the gift(s) but is not given the freedom to express it to the full glorification and edification of the Body.

The other case occurs when the individual is attempting to assume a role outside of his/her "calling." Because of a need for power, a need for recognition, or due to a misguided view of ministry, this person decides to proclaim for him or herself a certain type of ministry. Therefore, the individual assumes the role of "minister" using the societal definition. This particular person may be attracted to the aura and the perceived prestige of "ministry." Those factors may lead this person to embrace ministry in order to feel good psychologically or to garner a sense of importance. Such is done because the individual sees that role as providing a sense of self-actualization or the opportunity for other gains.

This issue or phenomenon is not unique or peculiar to the

"Black Church." Some "Black churches" may, however, be more vulnerable to having "ministers" without ministry due to additional factors beyond what has already been discussed. The first remains to be the ongoing reduced opportunity structure for persons to exemplify their skills and talents in the larger society due to racism, discrimination, and other limiting factors. Secondly, this may occur, as described earlier, when in fact the person has a ministry (skills, talents, gifts) but the church itself is not so structured so as to utilize these skills. This latter situation is one that will become more serious as time passes and more and more individuals acquire skills that the "Black Church" can use for the edification of the Body.

When reference is made to skills, I am referring to proficiencies that a person possesses; these skills may have been acquired through training, education, and/or experience. By talents, I am referring to those things that a person possesses which seem unique to them and appear to have been naturally acquired. On the other hand, gifts refer to the enablement that the Holy Spirit has given to individuals (see Romans 12:6–8; 1 Corinthians 12:1–11) for the edification of the Body of Jesus Christ (the church). Gifts in contrast to skills and talents are not naturally acquired. According to Scripture, each individual Christian has at least one spiritual gift. There are now instruments that have been developed to help an individual discern his or her spiritual gift(s). One such instrument was developed by Wagner (2005).

As the educational levels of congregations increase, it will be imperative that pastors and church administrators systematically and deliberatively make use of the array of acquired skills, along with spiritual gifts to the edification of the Body of Christ.

REALIZING THE FULL POTENTIAL
(A CHRISTIANITY/SPIRITUAL CHECK-UP)

How then can the tremendous work already performed by the church community be enhanced? To realize the full potential, individuals and congregations can do a "spiritual check-up." Just as a mental status exam is used in the psychological area, one can employ a "spiritual status exam" in the spiritual area. In the psychological area, to assess one's mental status one looks at a person's orientation to time and space, the adequacy of their memory (long- and short-term), their insight, their ability to make sound judgment, and the ability for sound reasoning. In the spiritual area, one can assess the following:

- Do I have an accurate and proper sense of history?
- Am I attempting to serve two masters?
- Is Christianity a way of life?
- Do I properly understand the biblical definition of ministry?
- Is Jesus Christ Savior *and* Lord?
- Is my conception of what a church is accurate?
- Is my overall theology biblically sound?
- Have I been truly "born again"?
- Is the congregation that I am involved in practicing the elements of a "highly effective" church (Barna 1999) and a "high impact" church (Barna and Jackson 2004a)?
- Can I detect a toxic faith system?
- Do I understand the role and ministry of the Holy Spirit in the Christian life?
- Is the congregation that I am a part of doing the work of the ministry or is it just "churching"?
- Am I growing in love as Jesus Christ commanded?

205

FINAL SUGGESTION

I would offer one final suggestion. Given the critical role the church continues to occupy in the lives of individuals and the dangers of "innocent" but detrimental concepts and programs operating in the church setting, I recommend that congregations should include born-again spiritually mature psychologists, counselors, and mental health professionals as part of their "ministry" staff. After being properly selected, their role would be to help plan and to examine the activities of the congregation and what occurs within so as to maximize the "psychological" growth of members—for true spirituality will include good psychology.

CONCLUSION

To realize its full potential, the church must be ministry-centered and teaching-oriented, emphasizing development and disciplining of men and women, focusing on its own survival as well as helping others. In an attempt to meet the broad range of needs in the congregation, they must be welcoming and open to utilizing the skills of everyone, including "professionals." Furthermore, the church would be wise to offer a variety of workshops, institutes, etc., to promote training and advancement on an ongoing basis. The harvest truly remains ripe. Will those who claim membership in the "church" be workers/ "ministers"? That is the question.

REFERENCES

Barna, G. (1999). *The Habits of Highly Effective Churches*. Ventura: Regal.

Barna, G. (2004b). Ethnic Groups Differ Substantially on Matters of Faith. http://www.barna.org.

Barna, G. (2004c). Beliefs of African Americans. http://www.barna.org.

Barna, G. and H. R. Jackson Jr. (2004a). *High Impact African American Churches*. Ventura: Regal.

Current Population Statistics (March 2002). U.S. Census Bureau. http://www.census.gov/cps.

Gallup, G. Jr. and T. Jones (2000). *The Next American Spirituality: Finding God in the Twenty-First Century*. Colorado Springs: Chariot Victor Publishing.

Keller, R. R. (2000). *Religious Diversity in North America*. In Richards, P. S. and A. E. Bergin, *Handbook of Psychotherapy and Religious Diversity*. Washington, D.C.: American Psychological Association.

King, M. L. K. Jr. (1998). "Guidelines for a Constructive Church." In Carson, C. and P. Holloron (Editors). *A Knock At Midnight: Inspiration from the Great Sermons of Reverend Martin Luther King, Jr*. New York: Time Warner.

Lincoln, C. and L. H. Mamiya (1990). *The Black Church in the African American Experience*. Durham: Duke University Press.

Menninger, K. (1973). *Whatever Became of Sin?* New York: Hawthorn Books.

Wagner, C. P. (2005). *Small Group Study Guide. Your Spiritual Gifts Can Help Your Church Grow—Updated and Expanded*. Ventura: Gospel Light.

CHAPTER 11

From Beautiful Buildings to a Beautiful Church

*"Upon this rock I will build
my church; and the gates of hell
shall not prevail against it."*
MATTHEW 16:18

*"Jesus saith unto her, Woman, believe me, the hour cometh, when
ye shall neither in this mountain, nor yet at Jerusalem, worship the
Father . . . But the hour cometh, and now is, when the true
worshippers shall worship the Father in spirit and in truth: for the
Father seeketh such to worship him. God is a Spirit: and they that
worship him must worship him in spirit and in truth."*
JOHN 4:21, 23–24

*"Let us hold fast the profession of our faith without wavering;
(for he is faithful that promised;) And let us consider one another
to provoke unto love and to good works: Not forsaking the
assembling of ourselves together; as the manner of some is;
but exhorting one another: and so much the more,
as ye see the day approaching."*
HEBREWS 10:23–25

*"That he might present it to himself a glorious church,
not having spot, or wrinkle, or any such thing;
but that it should be holy and without blemish."*
EPHESIANS 5:27

INTRODUCTION

Our Savior and Lord, Jesus Christ, proclaimed in Matthew 16:18 that "upon this rock I will build my church; and the gates of hell shall not prevail against it." The purposes of this chapter are to discuss the meaning of the word "church" as used in the New Testament; to explore some of the criticisms that have resulted from the misuse of its meaning; and to suggest ways in which one can move toward maximizing this powerful entity (organism).

THE WORD "CHURCH" AND THE BIBLE

The biblical word in Greek for church is "ekklesia," and means a calling out or a called out assembly (Strong, 1996). As such, the biblical church includes all those who have professed a faith in Jesus Christ as Savior and Lord.

Douglas (1971) said the following in regard to the term "church":

The English word "church" is derived from the Gk. Adjective *kyriakos* as used in some such phrases as *kriakon doma* or *kyriake oikia*, meaning "the Lord's house," *i.e.*, a Christian place of worship. "Church" in the New Testament, however, renders Gk. '*ekklesia*,' which mostly means a local congregation of Christians and never a building (p. 228).

Thus the term "church" has a very precise and unique meaning. Jesus Christ set out to build an inclusive community based on faith in Him and obedience to the Word of God. He never set out to establish a building. In the New Testament, there are various descriptions of the church. Among them are the body of Christ (Ephesians 4:12), the bride of Christ (Revelation 21:9), and the Lamb's wife (Revelation 21:9).

However, with the building spree, the real meaning of the church is often blurred and obscured. In history, building sprees are not unprecedented. Initially, with the formation of the New Testament church, there were not church buildings as such; rather, people went from house to house worshiping and fellowshipping. However, beginning in the third century AD, there evolved an emphasis on spectacular buildings. With this emphasis and the passage of time, the use of names other than "church" to describe these buildings also came into being. For many, the buildings have become equated with the church. One need only observe the language we use to see this demonstrated. For example, below are some common phrases in reference to the church which are inconsistent with the biblical concept:

- Let's go to church.
- Come to church with me.
- Invite someone to church.
- In my church . . .
- Where is your church located?

It has been estimated that in the United States there are some 320,000 protestant church buildings (Barna, 2004), of which 75,000 are considered to be predominantly Black congregations (Kunjufu, 1994). What we see now is a recurrence of the emphasis on buildings which can diminish a focus on what is really the church.

Many have criticized the overemphasis on buildings, particularly as spectacular edifices. For illustrative purpose of these criticisms, references will be made to comments by James Weldon Johnson (co-composer of what has come to be called the Black National Anthem, "Lift Every Voice and Sing"). Johnson had much to say about the church and its emphasis on buildings. For example, in an April 13, 1915, article (see Wilson, 1995, p. 140) entitled "Pagan Temples" he said:

> Some months ago we said in one of our articles that if Christ came to New York, we doubt if whether he would make his home in one of the pagan temples erected in his name. No doubt, some of our readers considered the statement irreverent. We had no intention of being flippant or irreverent; we meant exactly what we said.
>
> A short while ago one of the congregations of this city decided to erect a new church building at a cost of three million dollars. Later, it was decided to increase the cost to four million, two hundred thousand dollars. It is easy to understand why four million or more dollars might be put into an art museum or a public library or any other building built for show as much as for use, but what reason or excuse can be given for putting that amount of money into a church building? A church building should be comfortable and commodious; its beauty should be the beauty of simplicity and dignity.
>
> Four million dollars to build a church where a strong man, standing on one of its towers could hurl a baseball into the midst of poverty and human suffering. Four million dollars to build a church in the name of Him who founded the Christian religion as He trod his way from town to town. Four million dollars to rear a glittering temple in the name of Him who was the humblest among men; in the name of Him who had no

where to lay His head; in the name of Him who chose to live and labor among the lowly. It is mockery!

What will such a building stand for? It will stand for pride. Pride of the congregation, pride of the city. Pride, that is it! Worldly pride, the thing most directly opposed to the very essence of all Christ's teachings . . .

There you have an answer to the question, "What is the matter with the Church?" There you have a reason for the fact that the church is again losing its power over men's souls. Its strength is being spent in producing gorgeous flowers and delicate perfumes.

In another article (see Wilson, 1995, pp. 142–43) dated October 14, 1915, titled "What's the Matter with the Church?" Johnson stated:

The church is supposed to deal in spiritual things, but it charges hard cash. It is money, money, always money. There is no longer such a thing as free gospel, unless it is picked up on the street corners. And for what purpose is this money gathered? Does it go to feed the hungry? To clothe the naked? To care for the widow and the orphan? To some extent, yes; but the great bulk of it goes to maintain costly temples.

Does this bear any resemblance to what Jesus taught by word and example? Not the least. He founded the Christian religion as He walked along the shores of the Sea of Galilee, preaching to the crowds that gathered to hear Him. If Christ came to New York today, He could hardly be conceived as making His headquarters in one of the glittering, pagan temples erected to His name.

One of the most pronounced attributes of Christ was His sublime simplicity, his disdain of pomp and glory; the church today needs a new baptism of Christ-like simplicity.

This admonition applies not only to the church as a body, but to the ministry as individuals. Too many preachers have gone after the flesh pots of Egypt, too many have hungered after wealth, preferment and social position; and, thereby, lost their spiritual influence over the hearts of men. . . .

It is a psychic truth that the only kind of a man who can give out spiritual inspiration is a man of sincere simplicity; whether he does his preaching on a street corner or from gilded pulpit. And so the ministry also, in order to regain its spiritual influence over the hearts of men, needs a new baptism of Christ-like simplicity.

The above remarks are very harsh, however, Johnson overall respected the true church and wanted it to be and to do better as the following quote from a February 8, 1917, editorial (see Wilson, 1995, p. 145) titled "Responsibilities and Opportunities of the Colored Ministry" conveyed: "The most complete and powerful organization in the race is the Negro church. No other medium that we have can compare with the church in strength of appeal, breadth of influence and finality of authority."

Bowman and Hall (2000) in the book entitled *When Not to Build—An Architect's Unconventional Wisdom for the Growing Church* stated the following in the chapter titled "The Myth of Sacred Space":

All my life I had heard that the church building, especially the sanctuary, was "God's house" . . .

For the first time I realized no human could ever design a sanctuary. No amount of money, no amount of stained glass and carpet and padded pews could transform bricks and mortar into the dwelling place of God. God has already chosen his

213

dwelling place and he has chosen not "man-made temples" but the hearts of his people.

. . . my Bible study showed me that the New Testament church owned no church buildings, though they held both large-group and small-group meetings.

For almost three centuries the church built few if any buildings, and it continued to enjoy the most vigorous period of ministry and growth the church has ever known. Then disaster struck. Constantine declared Christianity the state religion. The church became less and less a community of believers, more and more a religious institution. The church built more and more buildings. Its focus had shifted. The church's most dynamic era had come to an end.

I found it hard to admit my mistakes, to concede that that much of my life's work had been misguided.

I came to see that unbiblical attitudes toward church buildings were among the greatest barriers to ministry and church growth in our time.

After what I had learned, I could no longer champion the sanctuary—space designed for worship only. I began to recommend instead what I call a "ministry center," a large area with a level floor and moveable furnishings that can be used not only for corporate worship but also for a host of other ministry activities throughout the week. In short, I quit viewing church buildings as sacred space and started seeing them, designing them, as tools for ministry (pp. 40–44).

Buildings clearly have a place in the life of Christians, but buildings are just the place that people congregate for various purposes. When buildings are built, they are constructed for the convenience of the congregations—not God. Buildings can be dedicated to the glory of God, but only the "born-again" people who are in that fellowship constitutes the true church in the biblical sense of the word.

MAKING BUILDINGS A BEAUTIFUL CHURCH

How then might we move from an overemphasis on building beautiful buildings to an emphasis on building beautiful churches? How can we get rid of or resolve what some have called the "edifice complex"? By "edifice complex," I mean a belief that to have a successful ministry and "church" one must have or build a beautiful building. Critical to getting rid of or resolving the "edifice complex" is adopting a proper view on what is really the church. Thus if one embraced the biblical concept of church, this would be the critical first step.

What else is needed in order to move from an emphasis on beautiful buildings to an emphasis on beautiful churches? One way of answering this question is to consider what comprises/makes up a beautiful building and then consider what would be the parallel for a beautiful church. If we were to outline what a beautiful building would consist of, we would probably agree on the following:

- a solid foundation
- high-efficiency central air conditioning system
- wall-to-wall carpeting
- a high-efficiency heating system
- beautiful and appropriate furniture
- numerous bathrooms
- adequate classroom space
- excellent acoustics and a state-of-the-art sound system
- a well-designed landscape plan so that there would be beautiful grass, shrubs, and trees
- appropriate lighting and fixtures

In constructing a beautiful building, one would be careful to select a competent architect and a competent contractor. One would also carefully embark on a sound financial plan. To build (be/become) a beautiful church, one needs to plan for this as concisely as one does when building a building. Unfortunately, this is too often not done.

Biblically speaking, since a building is not the church, to be a beautiful church the focus must be on winning and developing people in reference to their relationship with Jesus Christ. Hence, a beautiful church would consist of the following, at a minimum:

- a solid foundation with Jesus Christ as Lord
- a high-efficiency heating and cooling system (reliance on the Holy Spirit)
- wall-to-wall love (toward God, toward fellow humanity, and toward self)
- numerous programs designed to develop all age groups
- a focus on teaching and discipleship
- a focus on stewardship
- an emphasis on witnessing
- outreach and assistance to the needy
- a focus on justice and the elimination of injustices

CONCLUSION

Jesus Christ has given to His body, which is the church, the Holy Spirit; hence, we have the power to be as beautiful as the building in which we assemble. However, this will require obedience to the Word and the same careful attention that is given to creating the physical building.

REFERENCES

Barna, G. (January 12, 2004). Only Half of Protestant Pastors Have a Biblical Worldview. Barna Research Online. http://www.barna.org.

Bowman, R. and E. Hall (2000). *When Not to Build—An Architect's Unconventional Wisdom for the Growing Church (Expanded Edition)*. Grand Rapids: Baker Books.

Douglas, J. D. (1971). *The New Bible Dictionary*. Grand Rapids: W. B. Eerdmans.

Johnson, J. W. (Editor) (April 13, 1915). "Pagan Temples." In Wilson, S. K. (1995) *The Selected Writings of James Weldon Johnson. Vol. 1, The New York Age Editorials (1914–1923)*. New York, NY: Oxford University Press.

Johnson, J. W. (October 14, 1915). "What's the matter with the Church?" In Wilson, S. K. (Editor) (1995). *The Selected Writings of James Weldon Johnson. Vol. 1, The New York Age Editorials (1914–1923)*. New York, NY: Oxford University Press.

_____ (February 8, 1917). "Responsibilities and Opportunities of the Colored Ministry." In Wilson, S. K. (Editor) (1995). *The Selected Writings of James Weldon Johnson. Vol. 1, The New York Age Editorials (1914–1923)*. New York, NY: Oxford University Press.

Kunjufu, J. (1994). *Adam! Where are You? Why Most Black Men Don't Go to Church*. Chicago: African American Images.

Strong, J. (1996). *The New Strong's Exhaustive Concordance of the Bible*. Nashville: Thomas Nelson.

CHAPTER 12

Resources to Assist in Realizing the Church's Full Potential

"And the LORD answered me, and said,
Write the vision, and make it plain upon tables,
that he may run that readeth it."

HABAKKUK 2:2

■

"All scripture is given by inspiration of God,
and is profitable for doctrine, for reproof,
for correction, for instruction in righteousness."

2 TIMOTHY 3:16

Introduction

All of the sources quoted throughout this book can, in one way or the other, be useful as aids in assisting individuals and congregations to realize their full potential. However, in this final chapter, I will highlight some of these as well as suggest others. The listing of resources will be by broad categories and will include a brief description of each of the listings. Some of the books mentioned are no longer in print, but can be accessed through various libraries.

COUNSELING

- June, L. N., S. Black, and W. Richardson (Editors) (2002). *Counseling for Seemingly Impossible Problems—A Biblical Perspective* (formerly titled *Counseling in African American Communities: Biblical Approaches to Tough Issues.* Grand Rapids: Zondervan.

   This book provides a forum for practitioners in the field to discuss sixteen critical areas that counselors and parishioners may face. The areas covered are gambling addiction, sexual addiction, substance and domestic abuse, divorce, blended families, depression and bipolar disorders, schizophrenia, attention deficit hyperactive disorder, suicide, grief and loss, conflicts, health faith, demonology, unemployment, and research.

- Lee, C.C. (2005). *Multicultural Issues in Counseling: New Approaches to Diversity (Third Edition).* Alexandria: American Counseling Association.

  This edited volume will give the reader a good overview of multicultural counseling techniques and issues with various populations. One of the chapters deals specifically with the "African American Church."

- Walker, C. (1992). *Counseling with African Americans.* Grand Rapids: Zondervan.

  As one of the earlier books on counseling African American Christians, it provides a model for counseling.

FAMILY ISSUES

- Abatso, G. and Y. Abatso (1991). *How to Equip the African American Family.* Chicago: Urban Ministries, Inc.

  This is an excellent resource book on working with African American families.

- Finner-Williams, P. M. and R. D. Williams (2001). *Marital Secrets: Dating, Lies, Communication and Sex.* Detroit: RP Publishing.

  This book was written by a husband and wife team who shares both their therapeutic and legal experiences; they offer spiritual insights and helpful aids to those who are single, engaged, or married.

- June, L. N. (Editor) (1991). *The Black Family—Past, Present and Future.* Grand Rapids: Zondervan.

  This book provides a comprehensive overview of the African American family and offers concrete suggestions as to how to work with various issues in a positive manner.

• McAdoo, H. (Editor) (2007). *Black Families (Fourth Edition)* Thousand Oaks: Sage Publications.

> This edited and comprehensive work contains several chapters on various issues related to Black families. Included in this volume is a section titled, "Spirituality and Religion in Black Families." It also contains several chapters related to the religious dimensions.

• Richardson W. (1996). *Reclaiming the Urban Family: How to Mobilize the Church as a Family Training Center.* Grand Rapids: Zondervan.

> This book was written by a pastor of a very successful and progressive congregation. It presents tips and ideas on how to work systematically with the urban family using the local congregation as the base of operation.

MEN ISSUES

• June, L. N. and M. Parker (Editors) (1996). *Men to Men.* Grand Rapids: Zondervan.

> A handbook of issues faced by African American males. This edited work contains the thoughts of African American Christian men who are writing to African American men on issues of critical importance.

• Kunjufu, J. (1994). *Adam! Where are You? Why Most Black Men Don't Go to Church.* Chicago: African American Images.

> This is a valuable resource regarding some factors that lead some Black men to not attend church services. It is based on focus group conversations with African American males.

- Parker, M. (2002). *Teaching our Men/Reaching our Fathers*. Chicago: Lift Every Voice (Moody Publishers).

  This book represents the "wisdom" of one who has worked for years with African American men and discusses ways to effectively reach and teach men and fathers.

WOMEN ISSUES

- Carter, N. and M. Parker (1996). *Women to Women*. Grand Rapids: Zondervan.

  This book was released in tandem with *Men to Men* (see above) and presents the thoughts of African American Christian women who are writing to African American women on issues of critical importance.

HISTORY

- Diop, C.A. (1974). *The African Origin of Civilization—Myth or Reality*. Westport: Lawrence Hill.

  This book provides a good overview of Africa's contributions to civilization. It clearly shows that ancient Egyptian civilization was indeed of Black origin.

- DuBois, W. E. B. (1899). *The Philadelphia Negro—A Social Study*. Philadelphia: University of Pennsylvania Press.

  This book deals comprehensively with the lives of African Americans in the city of Philadelphia. It is considered a sociological classic. Sections 31–34 of chapter 12 deal with the church.

- Frazier, E. F. and C. E. Lincoln (1974). *The Negro Church in America: The Black Church Since Frazier.* New York: Schocken Books.

   This two-volume book represents the writing of two sociologists: E. Franklin Frazier and C. Eric Lincoln. The book represents two different time periods in the life of the church. Both are essential to understanding the evolving "Black Church" in America.

- Lincoln, C. E. and L. Mamiya (1990). *The Black Church in the African American Experience.* Durham: Duke University Press.

   This work represents probably the most comprehensive empirical study of the African American Church.

- Mays, B. E. and J. W. Nicholson (1933). *The Negro Church.* New York: New York Universities Press.

   For those interested in the development of the "Black Church" over time, this is also a must.

- McCray, W. A. (1990a). *The Black Presence in the Bible.* Volume 1. Chicago: Black Light Fellowship.

   This book and the one directly below show in detail the presence and involvement of Blacks in the Bible. It is a must read for those who do not understand or appreciate the contributions of Blacks to the development of the Old Testament faith which evolved into Christianity.

- _____ (1990b). *The Black Presence in the Bible and the Table of Nations.* Volume 2. Chicago: Black Light Fellowship.

   See description above.

• Walker, W. T. (1979). *Somebody's Calling My Name: Black Sacred Music and Social Change*. Valley Forge: Judson Press.
> This book is unique in that, in the words of the author, (see the Author's Preface) it "provides a general socio-historical introduction to Black Sacred Music, the roots of which are identified with the oral traditions of West Africa."

• Williams, C. (1976). *The Destruction of Black Civilization*. Chicago: Third World Press.
> This book attempts to show both the contributions of Blacks in history generally in addition to what has happened to Black civilizations over time. The area of Christianity is also discussed.

Evangelism and Discipleship

• June L. N. and M. Parker (1999). *Evangelism and Discipleship in African American Churches*. Grand Rapids: Zondervan.
> This book contains the thoughts of experienced Christians who are sharing their views on how to effectively evangelize and disciple Christians. The book is divided into five sections: History of African-American Evangelism, Taking the Lead in Evangelism and Discipleship, Training Laborers for Evangelism and Discipleship, Practicing Evangelism and Discipleship at Home and College, and Going into the Field.

Organizations

• Christian Research and Development.
> This organization is devoted to "improving your quality of life through training." Conferences, workshops, and training sessions are held annually. Numerous ma-

terials and publications are available. The address is: 27 W. Township Line Road, Suite 2, Upper Darby, Pennsylvania. 19082. The website address is: http://www. crdonline.org.

- Institute for Black Family Development.

    Headquartered in Detroit, Michigan, this institute focuses on Black family development. Over the years the Institute has developed a variety of materials that are helpful to churches and pastors in evangelism and discipleship. The mailing address is: 15151 Faust, Detroit, Michigan 48223. The phone number is: 313-493-9962. The web address is: www.ifbfd.org.

- Church Growth Unlimited.

    Dr. Lloyd C. Blue heads this organization. Dr. Blue is a former pastor who now devotes his time to working with pastors on church growth issues and expository preaching. The address is: P.O. Box 764305, Dallas, Texas 75376-4305.

- Christian Stronghold Baptist Church.

    Located in Philadelphia, Pennsylvania, this is one of several model churches nationally in regard to holistic ministries. The church is also a model in reaching and developing men. The church's motto is "Glorifying Christ, Amplifying the Bible and Edifying People Through Cells." The church is located at 4701 Lancaster Avenue, Philadelphia, Pennsylvania 19132. The phone number is: 215-877-1530. Dr. Willie Richardson is pastor. I highlight this congregation because I am familiar with its ministry. After having included this congregation at an earlier stage of writing this book, I was pleased to later find that it is highlighted in the book *High Impact African-American Churches* (2004) listed below that is coauthored by George Barna and Harry H. Jackson Jr.

- National Biblical Counseling Association.

    The National Biblical Counseling Association (NBCA) is, according to its mission statement, "a Christian organization that exists to provide excellence in biblical counseling through training, the study of God's Word, educational resources, and research." An annual conference is held. Its membership is primarily African American and is open to all. Information regarding the association may be obtained online from the following website: http://www.crdonline.org. On the homepage, click on NBCA.

- Black African-American Christian Counselors.

    This is a division of the American Association of Christian Counselors. It is composed of Black Christian counselors, social workers, counselors, or therapists. Its website materials state that "as the world and communities change, the demands for cultural competency also increase. Whatever your setting, you're sure to acquire valuable cultural sensitivity by joining BAACC, the newest division of the American Association of Christian Counselors. BAACC conferences and publications bring together the best of behavioral sciences with Christ-centered care. Learn about, and share, effective counseling techniques, expertise and culturally sensitive therapeutic models to assist those who counsel Black African Americans. Meet Christian counselors from diverse cultural and racial backgrounds." The website address is: http://www.aacc.net. Then click on baacc.

• The Barna Group.

> This organization conducts research on the church and publishes periodical reports. It is an excellent source of information on Christians and their belief systems. It also contains information on religious trends. Occasionally very valuable research is reported on Black Christians. The website is: www.barna.org

GENERAL

• Barna, G. and H. R. Jackson Jr. (2004). *High Impact African-American Churches*. Ventura: Regal.

> This unique book written by a White researcher and an African American pastor provides a valuable look at elements of "effective" "African American churches." Congregations that are interested in "best practices" will find this book very valuable. An additional value of the book is that it profiles eight "African American congregations" that are exemplary in eight areas of ministry and that would fit their definition of "high impact" churches.

• Taylor, R. J., L. M. Chatters and J. Levin (2004). *Religion in the Lives of African Americans—Social, Psychological, and Health Perspectives*. Thousand Oaks: Sage Publications.

> This book is a valuable resource in that it summarizes a wealth of data that have been collected over approximately twenty years. It contains data that show the effects of religion on the social, psychological, and health dimensions of African American individual and family lives.

EPILOGUE

The first draft of this book was outlined twenty-five years ago. It was not completed earlier because, as I would get back to it, other projects took precedence. Hence, the other four books that I have edited or coedited preceded this work.

However, as I reflect over that period of time, I am glad it was delayed. I often wonder what this book, if completed then, may have looked like twenty-five years ago. Over this period of time, some of my thinking and analyses have changed, new research has been done, additional books have been published, and new theoretical approaches have been advanced.

What this reflection over time has caused me to do is to see this book in its proper perspective. That is, it is simply one book written during a period of time. Twenty-five years from now there will be new issues and new challenges. Hopefully, however, this contribution will serve as one valuable addition regarding the church situation with a unique psychological emphasis and serve as a basis for further and more fuller treatise of this critical institution/organism.

"A Steady Beat," as reflected in the song written by James Weldon Johnson and R. Rosamond Johnson, has been the condition of Blacks of African descent in general as well as the function of the institutional "Black/African American Church."

As we continue our journey, may we continue the steady beat and may we continue to be "true to God and to our native land."

INDEX OF NAMES

ISBN-10: 0-8024-1138-X
ISBN-13: 978-0-8024-113-8

Exile. Persecution. Torture. The riveting story of one man's escape from the Sudan. By the muddy banks of the Kulo-jobi River, a young Sudanese boy is faced with a decision that will shape the rest of his life.

William Levi was born in southern Sudan as part of a Messianic Hebrew tribal group and spent the majority of his growing up years as a refugee running from Islamic persecution. He was eventually taken captive for refusing to convert to Islam and suffered greatly at the hands of his captor

by William O. Levi
Find it now at your favorite local or online bookstore.
www.LiftEveryVoiceBooks.com

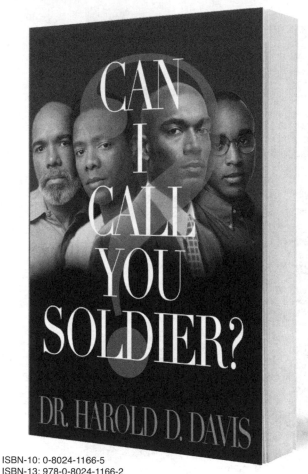

ISBN-10: 0-8024-1166-5
ISBN-13: 978-0-8024-1166-2

The war is at home and the battlefield is in the lives of our young men. In any community, and particularly in the black community, millions of young men feel the void of a role model. For every absent father, complacent leader, and passive bystander, there is a man who will step in and be a father figure—whether he is a trustworthy man of God or a dangerous enemy, someone will fill the void. It's up to us to win this battle and prepare the next generation to join in the fight. For the many men wondering how to win…*Can I Call You Soldier?* will be their strategy for victory.

by Dr. Harold Davis
Find it now at your favorite local or online bookstore.

www.LiftEveryVoiceBooks.com

ISBN-10: 0-8024-8801-3
ISBN-13: 978-0-8024-8801-5

Strengthen your future. Empower your family. Improve your finances. These are the ministry goals of Lee Jenkins, Registered Investment Advisor, financial speaker, and author of Taking Care of Business. In his new book, Jenkins answers the most common questions he is asked at his financial conferences. He combines biblical wisdom, financial deftness, empathy, and encouragement to create a powerful guide for people looking to improve their financial circumstances God's way.

by Lee Jenkins
Find it now at your favorite local or online bookstore.

www.LiftEveryVoiceBooks.com

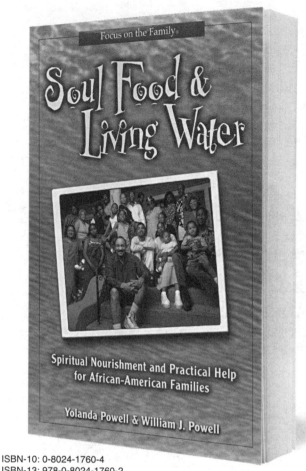

ISBN-10: 0-8024-1760-4
ISBN-13: 978-0-8024-1760-2

Overflowing with biblical teaching, practical examples and real encouragement, *Soul Food & Living Water* provides the spiritual nourishment the African-American family needs. Written in culturally sensitive language reflecting a rich heritage and strong faith, this book refreshes and equips families for today's challenges.

"Finally! This is the one we've been waiting for. Practical, relevant and refreshing, Soul Food & Living Water *isn't just another family guidebook. We're talking about real-life answers for to-day's black family."*

~Andrae Crouch, Recording Artist

by William J. Powell and Yolanda L. Powell
Find it now at your favorite local or online bookstore.

www.LiftEveryVoiceBooks.com

ISBN-10: 0-8024-8989-3
ISBN-13: 978-0-8024-8989-0

In the eerie, classic television show *The Twilight Zone*, characters caught in the zone wanted nothing more than to return to normal life. Similarly, survivors of severe trauma fall into *The Trauma Zone* – a place they want to escape from, but can't. Some cannot move forward, feeling stuck and victimized by their past. Some cannot see the present, living in denial of what has happened. And others cannot learn from the past, repeating the same mistakes over and over. All of them find they can't cope with the overwhelming emotions that accompany trauma. Collins, a licensed psychologist with over 25 years experience in the healthcare field, believes there is a way out of the trauma zone and back to emotional health, a path he outlines in this practical, encouraging book.

by R. Dandridge Collins
Find it now at your favorite local or online bookstore.

www.LiftEveryVoiceBooks.com

The Negro National Anthem

Lift every voice and sing
Till earth and heaven ring,
Ring with the harmonies of Liberty;
Let our rejoicing rise
High as the listening skies,
Let it resound loud as the rolling sea.
Sing a song full of the faith that the dark past has taught us,
Sing a song full of the hope that the present has brought us,
Facing the rising sun of our new day begun
Let us march on till victory is won.

LIFT EVERY VOICE

So begins the Black National Anthem, by James Weldon Johnson in 1900. Lift Every Voice is the name of the joint imprint of The Institute for Black Family Development and Moody Publishers.

Our vision is to advance the cause of Christ through publishing African-American Christians who educate, edify, and disciple Christians in the church community through quality books written for African Americans.

Since 1988, the Institute for Black Family Development, a 501(c)(3) nonprofit Christian organization, has been providing training and technical assistance for churches and Christian organizations. The Institute for Black Family Development's goal is to become a premier trainer in leadership development, management, and strategic planning for pastors, ministers, volunteers, executives and key staff members of churches and Christian organizations. To learn more about The Institute for Black Family Development write us at:

The Institute for Black Family Development
15151 Faust
Detroit, Michigan 48223

We hope you enjoy this book from Moody Publishers. Our goal is to provide high-quality, thought-provoking books and products that connect truth to your real needs and challenges. For more information on other books and products written and produced from a biblical perspective, go to www.moodypublishers.com or write to:

Moody Publishers/LEV
820 N. LaSalle Boulevard
Chicago, IL 60610
www.moodypublishers.com